Competitive Judo

Ron Angus

Human Kinetics

Library of Congress Cataloging-in-Publication Data

Angus, Ron, 1956-
    Competitive judo / Ron Angus.
        p. cm.
    Includes index.
    ISBN 0-7360-5744-7 (soft cover)
    1. Judo. I. Title.
    GV1114.A96 2006
    796.815'2--dc22

                                                    2005017667

ISBN: 0-7360-5744-7   ` **3 1088 1004 5713 2**

Developmental Editor: Cynthia McEntire; **Assistant Editor:** Scott Hawkins; **Copyeditor:** Patsy Fortney; **Proofreader:** Sue Fetters; **Indexer:** Sue Fetters; **Graphic Designer:** Nancy Rasmus; **Graphic Artist:** Tara Welsch; **Photo Manager:** Dan Wendt; **Cover Designer:** Keith Blomberg; **Photographer (cover):** © DPPI-SIPA/Icon SMI; **Photographer (interior):** André Ringuette/ Freestyle Photography unless otherwise noted; **Printer:** United Graphics

Human Kinetics books are available at special discounts for bulk purchase. Special editions or book excerpts can also be created to specification. For details, contact the Special Sales Manager at Human Kinetics.

Printed in the United States of America   10 9 8 7 6 5 4 3 2 1

Human Kinetics
Web site: www.HumanKinetics.com

United States: Human Kinetics
P.O. Box 5076
Champaign, IL 61825-5076
800-747-4457
e-mail: humank@hkusa.com

Canada: Human Kinetics
475 Devonshire Road Unit 100
Windsor, ON N8Y 2L5
800-465-7301 (in Canada only)
e-mail: orders@hkcanada.com

Europe: Human Kinetics
107 Bradford Road
Stanningley
Leeds LS28 6AT, United Kingdom
+44 (0) 113 255 5665
e-mail: hk@hkeurope.com

Australia: Human Kinetics
57A Price Avenue
Lower Mitcham, South Australia 5062
08 8277 1555
e-mail: liaw@hkaustralia.com

New Zealand: Human Kinetics
Division of Sports Distributors NZ Ltd.
P.O. Box 300 226 Albany
North Shore City
Auckland
0064 9 448 1207
e-mail: info@humankinetics.co.nz

To my parents George and Amelia Angus for their untiring support throughout my life. And to my wife Tracy and daughter Chelsea Louise, who, thankfully, are my partners in all of life's great adventures.

Contents

Part I Techniques

Part II   Tactics and Strategy

Foreword

I am deeply honored that Ron Angus asked me to write the foreword to his amazing new book *Competitive Judo*. Ron has given the martial arts community a tremendous gift in writing this book. His dedication, knowledge, and continuous pursuit of excellence should earn him the title "National Treasure". I've had the pleasure of watching and learning from Ron for over 30 years. He has unselfishly shared his vast knowledge of Judo with all who are interested.

Because of my faith in him as a coach, I have sent many of my athletes to Ron for elite level training with absolutely amazing results. I highly recommend that all judo players, from beginning students to international competitors, study this book. It is an essential and valuable resource for every coach. I am a better student of the sport and a better coach because of Ron Angus.

Patrick Burris
1972 and 1978 Olympian
1996 USA Judo Team Olympic coach
Seven-time USA Judo national champion

Acknowledgments

It is my pleasure to acknowledge the individuals who assisted so generously in the completion of this book.

First I must thank my coauthor, Wally Watkins, who is my former high-school English teacher, my fellow clubmate in judo, and a great friend. He put in countless hours of work on this book and encouraged me with his support. Thank you to his wife Joan as well for her generous and unselfish gift of Wally's time.

I thank my judo friends whose help was only a phone call away: Tracy Angus, Pat Burris, Joe Serianni, Mike Flynn, Andrzej Sadej, Peter Edwards, Christopher Miller, and Maurice McDowell. Their technical advice and their willingness to be sounding boards are greatly appreciated.

My appreciation must be expressed to Human Kinetics and Ed McNeely for thinking of me when Human Kinetics decided to publish a book on competitive judo. Equally my thanks go out to Cynthia McEntire for leading me through the publishing process with such kindness and patience.

Finally, I thank my students for volunteering to be used as models for many of the photos used throughout this book: Fraser Bridgeman, Katy Bryant, Adrianna Fierastrau, Mary-Elizabeth Harvey, Jonathan Hilkewich, Alexander McKeown, and Mathew McKeown. Their dedication to training is what keeps me motivated as a coach.

Introduction

Competitive judo is an exciting, multifaceted sport that requires the fast hands of a boxer for obtaining a grip, the explosive power of an Olympic lifter for executing a throw, and the agility of a gymnast for maneuvering into and out of various attacking situations. Competitive judoka also need the aerobic and anaerobic fitness of both sprinters and long-distance runners to endure repeated bouts of high-intensity action during a match and recover from repeated high-intensity fights throughout each competition day.

In addition to these physical requirements, competitive judoka must have the tactical awareness of master chess players and the ability to strategize tactical plans so as to prepare for competition against multifaceted opponents who have different styles, body types, strengths, and weaknesses. Moreover, they must be able to keep a cool head in the heat of competition.

This book is intended as a blueprint for intermediate and advanced judoka to use to achieve this level of success; it provides reinforcement and support as they prepare physically, mentally, and tactically for match competition. Keep in mind that the main objective of sport judo is to gain ippon (total victory). This book will help you reach that level.

The variety of challenges presented by the sport is what makes competitive judo so addictive for elite judoka. The European Judo Union stated that judo was the second-most-watched event on European television during the first week of the Athens Olympic Games.

Throughout this book, I emphasize that there is no right or wrong way to do judo. However, there are, depending on your own strengths and weaknesses, more or less efficient ways of doing judo. Your strategies and techniques need only fall within the basic rules and principles of judo. Fortunately, the rules of judo are designed to encourage constant growth and experimentation with new and exciting ways of applying the basic principles of judo that the founder, Jigoro Kano, derived from the fighting art of jujitsu before 1886—the controlling or manipulation of an opponent sufficiently enough to throw him flat on his back or subdue him on the ground.

Throughout my more than 40 years in judo, first as a competitor and then a coach, the many facets of judo and the need for versatility have kept me fascinated. Kano was a gifted educator, and as any good teacher knows, the more input students have in their own education, the more they will learn and continue to study. The more each judoka studies, the more enriched the sport of judo itself becomes.

Kano's goal was to spread judo throughout the world not only as a sport but also as an educational tool. Kano's dream has been fulfilled: Not only is judo now practiced throughout the world, but it is also a truly international sport with each culture adding its own flavor. Close study of the cultural traits and strengths of the sport across the different nationalities reveals many different elements in both training and fighting methods.

The Japanese, with their preference for tradition and their extremely long workdays, train and compete in a fashion that mirrors their culture. They have very long training sessions and attempt to fit as much judo as possible into each 5-minute fight. The Russians use a much more scientific approach to the sport. They borrow from other grappling sports such as sombo and wrestling, while using untraditional tactics and fighting styles. These are the two extremes, but each member country of the International Judo Federation (IJF) borrows the skills and traits of the others, not only enhancing their own judo but also enriching judo as a sport through this morphing of styles. The recent successes of judoka in the ever-expanding field of mixed martial arts testify to the effectiveness of these developments outside the judo community.

Throughout the book, I cover the most common and effective skills used in modern competitive judo, including grips, setups, throws, transition moves, and ground techniques. These skills appear in the book in the order in which they are used in a contest. Each set of skills is referred to as a gateway. Once you complete a technique from each skill set, you step through a gateway into a room or field in which you can choose from a number of directions.

Sport judo training and conditioning today emphasize a smaller, modified, variable set of techniques that are decisive in competition and that have been adopted and adapted from classical judo. On this basis, this book examines the psychology of preparation and competition and the techniques, strategies, training, and tactics for high-level judo competition. Every section refers to the rules of the IJF and reiterates the need to study ways of using those rules, because the rules are the tools we use to win.

The first concern of the rules is to protect fighters. Even so, a respect for progression is implicit in the IJF rules to prevent stagnation of the sport. Rules shape tactics. Tactics require conditioning. The conditioned and tactically aware judoka interprets these rules. When those interpretations lead to negative developments in the sport, the IJF sometimes changes the rules.

The first chapter presents the rules of judo as a foundation on which elite judoka must build strategies for tactics and conditioning. This foundation, often neglected, introduces the tactical evolution as a background.

The ultimate goal of judo is to control the opponent. This is demonstrated by the ability to throw an opponent flat on his back, hold him in a controlled manner on his back for 25 seconds, or obtain a submission from the opponent by applying an effective armlock or choke. Ippon in any form begins with gripping and continues by controlling the opponent's body movement.

During a judoka's preparation, the techniques, tactics, and strategies are woven together to form a complete fighter. If strategies are the overall vision, then tactics are the tools to complete the strategies. Technical skills, tactics, and conditioning allow a judoka to carry out his match strategy.

I like to think of this book as a collection of weapons from which judoka can choose. The book coaches competitors about how to win at judo rather than how to improve the techniques they already know. As a tactical book rather than a technique book, *Competitive Judo* is based firmly on the rules and the scoring system of judo. From this base, competitors can apply rule-guided tactics to their favorite throwing, groundwork, and counter techniques.

Strength and conditioning are necessary elements when preparing for competition. Therefore, I included a chapter on each of the required types of strengths and conditioning to make you competitive. The book concludes with a discussion on mental preparation and setting up a match plan, which is crucial for success. Judo was founded on strategy, and match plans have always been used to enable judoka to pit their strengths against their opponents' weaknesses.

QUALITIES OF AN ELITE JUDOKA

What does it take to be an elite judoka? The standard answer would be winning or medaling at age-appropriate state, regional, and national events. The dedication of an athlete could also be measured by the time spent in training: perhaps 6 hours of judo a week at 14 to 16 years of age (depending on physical development) up to the level of an Olympian, who would require 12 or more hours of judo a week, not including off-mat training or other sport training for recreation or fitness. In all, senior national team members could end up training 20 hours a week.

Being an elite judoka requires, in a word, *tenacity*. For years judo coaches have been searching for that magical something that makes a judo champion. As far as I can tell, the one trait that all judo champions have is the tenacity to keep going—to keep training when they're too exhausted to train; to train while coping with the pressures of everyday life; and most important, to get up and keep fighting once they have been knocked down.

In all my years of judo I have never seen a better example of this tenacity than at the 1987 World Championships in Essen, Germany. In the preliminary rounds, the reigning world champion, Karen Briggs of Great Britain, fighting in the 48-kilogram (106-pound) division, spun in for her famous taiotoshi and broke her ankle. Everyone stood in amazement as Karen begged the British team doctor to instruct her how to reset her ankle so she could continue fighting. Luckily, Ken Kingsbury, the British team doctor, who always cared much more for his fighters than for their results, convinced Karen that the day was over, but that she would be back another day. And she did return. Karen came back to win the 1989 worlds in Belgrade, Yugoslavia.

Even a judoka with tenacity as great as Karen needs skill, conditioning, and support. Certainly it takes family support to become an elite judoka because a young judoka's family may make all the difference, especially with the financial support young adults need until they make the national team. In the same way, a competitor needs club support—a club or possibly a combination of clubs to meet the needed hours of training as well as a coach who has the expertise to supply well-balanced judo training.

Natural talent is also a factor, although the skills needed to fight judo are so varied that talent identification has not been particularly effective in judo. The ability to use individual strengths and the determination to improve weaker points seem to be the best indicators of successful future development in judo competition.

Each one of these factors is relevant, but the most useful definition of an elite athlete is a judoka who has the ability to focus on understanding and preparing tactics. For the purposes of this book, I suggest that an elite judoka is one who has achieved not only the basic skills but also an understanding of gateways and drills so as to become self-actualized and self-shaping in aspects of conditioning and tactics. Gateways and drills are part of the progression to tactics.

GATEWAYS

Judo has distinct stages of scrimmage. These form the total series of events between the referee saying "hajime" and "matte": gripping, circling to a throwing position, throwing, transitioning to groundwork, and finally, executing groundwork.

It helps to consider each stage a gateway. Once you have passed through the threshold of the gate, you have a number of options or directions for proceeding to the next gate.

The very essence of judo is in the training and the drills that enable you instinctively to choose an option or a direction in which to proceed, an option resulting from a combination of actions both you and your opponent have taken. If you choose a particular grip, say a sleeve collar grip, then think of that grip as a gate—once you get that grip, you cross over a threshold. Now you have a number of choices to make or other gates to choose from. These gates are the direction in which you can circle to set up uke for an entry into a throw. Once you have started the entry to the throw (more specifically, the direction of the throw), then comes the next group of choices or gates that you may go through. This process continues throughout the whole scrimmage until matte is called or ippon is awarded.

These decisions must be made instinctively and automatically. The most effective way to develop this instinct is skill repetition under increasingly difficult situations or increased resistance. A judoka can design drills that make these choices automatic by starting with the basic movements and then gradually adding changes and resistance.

The more automatically and efficiently you can pass through these gates, the more often you will find yourself in the desirable position of being one step or gate ahead of uke. Remember, you and your opponent may not be at the same gate.

If you find yourself one gate behind your opponent, it is advisable to cut the grip and start the whole process over rather than try to catch up. You must be one step ahead when you are maneuvering uke into a throwing position. This is particularly true when competitors are dealing with a grip, often they focus too long on the grip. Once the grip is obtained you must move on to the next gate. If you prepare and drill thoroughly, you can be two steps ahead and setting up the throw while your opponent is still at gate one trying to secure a grip.

You cannot combine gates or skip a gate, although sometimes a step is almost imperceptible. Even so, close analysis of a successful maneuver shows that all the necessary actions have been taken. Understanding the steps or gates of a complete sequence is the first step toward designing specific drills for developing a repertoire of tactics. Ensure that in your drill you include each gate and all the directions or choices inside the gate before you move through to the next gate.

DRILLS

Through drills, judoka develop the four stages or gateways of a judo match—grips, setups, throws, and groundwork—areas in which they create and seize tactical opportunities. The drills themselves are divided into four categories: individual skills, linking of skills, tactical use of linked skills, and judo-specific conditioning through the use of drills and controlled randori. These last three categories are areas in which elite athletes train continually.

It is important to notice the progression in this sequence. Drills may be distinguished from controlled randori by the fact that uke has a prearranged action plan during drills. Thus, in controlled randori, uke cooperates with tori to develop a particular skill or chain of skills. During controlled randori, tori and uke are put into specific situations with set parameters and then given freedom to react as they wish as long as they stay within those parameters.

Individual skill drills are designed to assist a judoka in learning individual skills such as a specific grip, a particular throw, or a chosen ground move. Skill-linking drills are designed to link a number of skills together such as two skills in sequence (for example, the transition to groundwork following a specific hold or armlock) or several skills in sequence proceeding right though the whole chain, from grips to groundwork, including all the steps in between.

Tactics are the backbone of winning in high-level judo competitions. Tactical drills use a number of linked skills to help the judoka practice reacting to specific situations or creating tactically advantageous situations.

Controlled randori can be used in any situation or all of the previous situations once the basic skills have been developed. Controlled randori should be the backbone for introducing or practicing situations for all athletes at the elite level so that they can invent, develop, and then extemporize their own unique solutions to the challenges of competitive judo.

Throughout my life, I have had the good fortune to visit many countries and to study with some of the world's greatest judoka. This book includes information that I gathered throughout those years. It my great wish that you use this book as a resource to find information and synthesize it into your existing judo to become a more complete competitive judoka. Just as this book brings together information gathered from the kind and generous fellow judoka who have shared their judo with me, I am sharing this information with you.

PART I

Techniques

1

IJF Rules
of Competition

The modern sport form of judo has evolved from having a martial art emphasis on traditions and philosophy to having an emphasis on match competition based on sport science and structured rules. Even in the form developed and taught by Jigoro Kano, some techniques were not practical or effective in a sport setting.

The legacy of Jigoro Kano continues through an evolving definition of sport judo. Although the transition from a traditional martial art form to match competition began very early, modern judo began with the first World Judo Championship in 1952. A process of ratification and acceptance continued with the inclusion of judo in the 1964 Olympic Games, particularly with the entry of the Eastern Bloc teams. The breakup of the Eastern European Communist Bloc after 1989 accelerated the development of the sport as greater numbers of Eastern Bloc competitors, whose fighting styles and training methods became standard, changed the styles and methods of sport-specific conditioning.

Understanding the rules and using them to your best advantage is part of any sport; judo is no exception. From the early days when judo was just another form of jujitsu, struggling for recognition as a separate art, Kano, judo's founder, wisely ensured that all matches against other styles of jujitsu were fought under the rules of kodokan judo. He also arranged for the matches to be fought on the slick surface of straw tatami so his fighters could use foot sweeps, giving them a large advantage over their opponents since foot sweeps were seldom used by the other fighting styles.

This chapter contains a summary of the IJF rules. In the first part, we will look at the rules as they pertain to the gateways judoka pass through during a match: grips, setups, throws, and groundwork. Next, we will consider some recent rule changes and how they have affected the sport. Finally, I will summarize the rules dictating the procedure and scoring system of a judo match. Throughout the book, you will find references to these rules. By learning the rules and connecting them to the skills, you will be able to design your own drills and conditioning programs.

An astute judoka understands the intent of the rules and works within these guidelines to achieve ippon. Although the rules continue to evolve, the intent of the rules stays the same. There are four main intentions basic to the rules of modern judo:

1. To protect the fighters from injury;
2. To give both judoka an equal and fair chance to apply their judo during a match in an attempt to achieve ippon;
3. To make judo a dynamic and spectator-friendly sport; and,
4. To encourage new and inventive ways to keep the sport of judo evolving and growing.

To fulfill these four main goals, the IJF periodically changes the rules or adds new rules. These changes are usually in response to the evolution of judo techniques or strategies that challenge or endanger one of the four basic goals of the rules.

If you wish to be truly competitive at judo, you must keep on top of the rules of judo and the occasional adaptations to the rules. This way, you and the referee will be looking for the same outcome or result in any given situation. For example, when taking your opponent into groundwork, you must demonstrate that you have taken uke down in a skillful manner or have capitalized on a failed attempt by uke. This is what the referee is looking for, and the successful judoka will stay within the boundaries of the rules in order to earn the highest score.

The concept of clearly demonstrating what the referee wants to see is not new. It was rumored that the extremely successful judo coach George Kerr of Scotland, who trained two-time Olympic gold medalist Peter Siesenbacher of Austria, used this tactic successfully throughout his coaching career. George, who was himself a retired top international fighter from Great Britain and also an IJF-A referee, kept a record on different top referees, identifying their favored techniques and fighting styles. When possible, George tried to work this information into his fighter's match plan as much as reasonably possible to achieve an added kinship or favor with the referee. The theory was simple: if the referee liked newaza, he might subconsciously allow a little longer time for a judoka to execute ground moves. Although this example seems extreme, the theory has merit. If you clearly demonstrate you are applying judo by

© Empics

The wise judoka learns the rules and applies them strategically to obtain ippon.

following the intent of the rules and giving the referee what he or she wants to see, you will be less likely to lose borderline judgment calls. The referee is more likely to give you the benefit of the doubt.

Remember, this is only a summary of the rules most important to a judoka. For a complete description of the rules, refer to the rules on the IJF's Web site at www.ijf.org.

Rules Governing Gateways

We can identify four gateways as being important parts of a judo scrimmage during a match: grips, setups, throws, and groundwork. Each of these gateways wil be covered in more detail later in the book. Take care to understand the rules as they apply to each of these gateways. Knowing how to work within the rules will take you through each gateway more smoothly, with fewer penalties and more chances for success.

Gateway: Grips

A judoka must have a clear understanding of the difference between orthodox and unorthodox grips. Simply stated, an orthodox grip is when tori's right hand is holding the left side of uke's jacket and tori's left hand is holding the right side of uke's jacket. Any deviation that falls within the permissible rule of gripping may be held for only 3 seconds. (See article 27, prohibited acts and penalties.)

Taking a high grip on the opponent's collar is regarded as normal even if the hand is gripping on the opposite side of the opponent's jacket, as long as the hand passes behind the opponent's head.

A contestant should not be penalized for holding with an abnormal grip if the situation has been brought about by his opponent ducking his head beneath the holder's arm. However, if a contestant is continually ducking this way, the referee should consider whether he is adopting an excessively defensive posture.

When designing your own gripping drills, remember the intent of the gripping rules—to give both judoka a fair chance to apply their judo. As long as you are applying an orthodox grip, you can make it difficult for uke to get his preferred grip. Try breaking uke's posture by bending him at the waist (sleeve lapel grip). Stop uke from getting a second hand on your gi by skillfully using a fanning or flicking action with the hand you are using to control uke's sleeve (sleeve lapel and sleeve collar grip). For more information on grips, see chapter 2.

Gateway: Setups

To avoid a passivity penalty, a judoka either must be actively avoiding his opponent's attacks or actively trying to set up his opponent for an attack. The referee must see the judoka actively setting up his opponent for attack while staying within the tactical rules of judo.

Because most setups should be performed continuously, flowing between the gateways of gripping and throwing, the setup is a great time to use unorthodox grips. The unorthodox grips provide the flow needed to get to the setup, allowing the judoka to then throw his opponent.

Setups must be thought of as a distinctive skill but should be trained as a link between grips and throws. When moving into setup position, try one-handed grips, unorthodox grips, fakes, blocks, stumbles, and combinations. See chapter 5 for more information on setups.

Gateway: Throws

To be counted as a proper throwing attack, tori must demonstrate control. For a throwing attack to be considered a legitimate attack, with no fear of a penalty for false attack, tori must demonstrate a clear intent to throw uke. Intent is demonstrated by the breaking of uke's posture as tori demonstrates a true attempt to complete a throw. (See article 27, prohibited acts and penalties.)

Attempting a throw such as haraigoshi or uchimata with only one hand gripping the opponent's lapel from a position resembling wakigatame (in which the wrist of the opponent is trapped beneath the thrower's armpit)

In a legal throw, tori demonstrates both control and intent.

and deliberately falling facedown onto the mat is likely to cause injury and will be penalized. Moves executed by a judoka not intending to throw the opponent cleanly onto his back are dangerous and will be treated in the same way as wakigatame.

When choosing throws to train, use the rating system described in chapter 3. Link the throws with a number of different setups. Although all judoka aspire to throw for ippon, it is valuable to study adapted throws so you can attempt to get lesser scores when needed. See blocks and stumbles in chapter 5.

Gateway: Groundwork

The transition into groundwork must be skillful. A judoka must use either a failed attack or action of the opponent or an incomplete attack or action of his own. The application of a ground skill must be immediate and fall within the guidelines for the rules of judo.

When selecting ground moves to drill, use the rating system in chapter 6. Link together throws and ground moves that create the most direct path from the throw to the ground skill. Try to develop a follow-up technique for each ground move you train.

Article 16 deals with entry into newaza. Contestants are allowed to change from standing position to newaza in the following cases:

- A contestant, after obtaining some result by a throwing technique, can change without interruption into newaza and take the offensive.
- When a contestant falls to the ground following the unsuccessful application of a throwing technique, the other contestant may take advantage of his opponent's unbalanced position to take him to the ground.
- When one contestant obtains some considerable effect by applying a shimewaza or kansetsuwaza in the standing position, he can then change without interruption to newaza.
- One contestant may take his opponent down into newaza by the particularly skillful application of a movement that does not qualify as a throwing technique.
- In any other case in which one contestant might fall down or be about to fall down, the other contestant may take advantage of the opponent's position to go into newaza.

Keep in mind, however, that if the employment of the technique is not continuous, the referee will order both contestants to resume the standing position.

When one contestant pulls his opponent down into newaza in a way that is not in accordance with the situations outlined in article 16 and his opponent does not take advantage of this to continue into newaza, the referee will announce matte, stop the contest, and award shido to the contestant who infringed article 27.

RULES GOVERNING MATCHES

The next section covers the rules dictating the procedures and scoring systems of a judo match. For a judoka to compete with ease, to be free flowing yet inventive, he must understand the rules and their intent and learn to fit his style within those rules. He must grow familiar with the rules and comfortable in his understanding of them. Setups for a situation are always orchestrated, although the final outcome is usually a surprise.

Uniform and Hygiene

Articles 3 and 4 of the IJF rules cover the appearance of the judoka during a contest. Article 3 outlines the uniform of the judoka, and article 4 covers personal hygiene.

Contestants shall wear judogi that are made of a strong material such as cotton and are in good condition (no tears). The material must not be so thick or so hard as to prevent the opponent from taking a grip. The first contestant wears a blue judogi, and the second contestant wears white or off-white.

The jacket should be long enough to cover the thighs and should at a minimum reach the fists when the arms are fully extended at the sides of the body. The body of the jacket is worn with the left side crossed over the right. It should be wide enough to provide a minimum overlap of 20 centimeters at the level of the bottom of the rib cage. The sleeves of the jacket must reach to the wrist joint as a maximum and 5 centimeters above the wrist joint as a minimum. A space of 10 to 15 centimeters needs to be between the sleeve and the arm (inclusive of bandages) on the entire length of the sleeve.

A contestant must wear a strong belt, 4 to 5 centimeters wide, of a color that corresponds to the contestant's grade. The belt is worn over the jacket at waist level and tied with a square knot that is tight enough to prevent the jacket from being too loose. The belt must be long enough to go twice around the waist and leave 20 to 30 centimeters protruding from each side of the knot when tied.

Under their jackets, female contestants may wear a plain white or off-white leotard with short sleeves. If they prefer, female contestants can wear their jackets tucked inside their trousers.

Article 4 states that the personal hygiene of a contestant must reach a high standard. Judogi must be clean and generally dry, and shouldn't smell bad. The nails of the feet and hands must be cut short. Long hair needs to be tied back to avoid causing inconvenience to the other contestant.

Any contestant who will not comply with the requirements of articles 3 and 4 will be refused the right to compete. The opponent will win the contest by kikengachi, according to the rule of the majority of three.

Contest Location and Duration

Article 9 concerns the location of the contest and the valid areas in which judoka may fight. The contest shall be fought in the contest area. Any technique applied when one or both contestants are outside the contest area will not be recognized. If a contestant has even one foot, hand, or knee outside the contest area while standing or more than half his body outside the contest area while doing sustemi waza, he will be considered outside the contest area.

There are some exceptions to the rule of staying within the contest area. When one contestant throws his opponent outside the contest area but stays within the contest area long enough for the effectiveness of the technique to be clearly apparent, the technique will be recognized. When a throw is started with both contestants inside the contest area, but during the throw the contestant being thrown moves outside the contest area, the action may be considered for point-scoring purposes if the throwing action continues uninterrupted and the contestant executing the throw stays within the contest area long enough for the effectiveness of the action to be clearly apparent. In newaza, the action is valid and may continue so long as either contestant has any part of the body touching the contest area. If during the course of an attack such as ouchigari or kouchigari, the foot or leg of the thrower leaves the contest area and moves over the mat of the safety area, the action will be considered valid for scoring purposes as long as the thrower does not place any weight on the foot or leg while it is outside the contest area.

Very stressful situations often occur when fighting on the edge of the mat. It is imperative to design drills that will make you familiar with these situations: putting your opponent at the edge of the mat or escaping yourself from the edge of the mat. You can reduce the mental stress of fighting on the edge of the mat by training your technical and tactical abilities to use these situations to your fullest advantage.

In the case of osaekomi on the edge, if the one part of the contestant still touching the contest area loses contact with the mat, the referee must announce matte. If tori becomes airborne (i.e., is no longer in contact with the mat) outside the contest area during the execution of a throw, the technique can be considered valid for scoring purposes only if uke lands before any part of tori touches outside the contest area.

Because the red danger zone is part of the contest area, any contestant whose feet are still touching the red danger zone in the standing position will be considered within the contest area.

During sustemi waza, a throw is considered valid if one half or more of the thrower's body is within the contest area. Therefore, neither foot of the thrower should leave the contest area before his back or hips touch the mat.

If the thrower falls outside the contest area while executing a throw, the action will be considered for scoring purposes only if the opponent's body touches the mat before the thrower's. If a thrower's knee, hand, or any other part of his body touches the safety area before his opponent's body, any result will be disregarded.

Once the contest starts, the contestants may leave the competition area only if the referee gives permission to do. Permission will be given only in very exceptional circumstances, such as the necessity to change a judogi that does not comply with article 3 or that has become damaged or soiled.

Article 10 concerns the duration of the contest. For the world championships and Olympic Games, the time duration of contests is 5 minutes of real contest time for both men and women with the possibility of up to 5 minutes of overtime (golden score). Any contestant is entitled to rest between contests for a period of 10 minutes.

Article 11 further expands on the duration of the contest. The time elapsed between the announcement of matte and hajime and between sono mama and yoshi by the referee does not count as part of the duration of the contest.

Article 13 concerns osaekomi time:

- Ippon: total of 25 seconds
- Wazari: 20 seconds or more but less than 25 seconds
- Yuko: 15 seconds or more but less than 20 seconds
- Koka: 10 seconds or more but less than 15 seconds

An osaekomi of less than 10 seconds will be counted the same as an attack.

Article 14 covers any technique coinciding with the time signal. Any immediate result of a technique started simultaneously with the time signal is considered valid. In the case of osaekomi announced simultaneously with the time signal, the time allotted for the contest shall be extended until either ippon is scored or the referee announces toketa or matte. The contest always begins in the standing position. Only members of the Referee Commission can interrupt the contest. (See article 17.)

Application of Matte

Article 17 deals with when the referee can and cannot call matte. The referee will announce matte to stop the contest temporarily in the following cases:

- When a contestant goes outside the contest area (see the exceptions listed in article 9)
- When a contestant performs one of the prohibited acts
- When a contestant is injured or taken ill
- When a contestant must adjust his uniform
- When there is no apparent progress during newaza
- When a contestant regains a standing or semistanding position from newaza while bearing his opponent on his back
- When a contestant lifts his opponent who is on his back clear of the mat, either during newaza or when regaining a standing position from newaza
- When a contestant performs or attempts to perform kansetsuwaza or shimewaza from the standing position and the result is not immediately apparent
- When in any other case the referee deems it necessary to do so
- When the referee and judges or Referee Commission wish to confer

To recommence the contest, the referee will announce hajime.

Having announced matte, the referee must take care to maintain the contestants within view, in case they do not hear the matte announced and continue fighting.

The referee should not call matte to stop a contestant from going outside the contest area unless the situation is considered dangerous. The referee should not announce matte when a contestant who has escaped (for example, osaekomi, shimewaza, kansetsuwaza) appears in need of or calls for a rest.

The referee should announce matte when a contestant who is facedown on the mat and has his opponent clinging to his back succeeds in rising to a half standing position with his hands clear of the mat. This indicates a loss of control by the opponent.

If the referee calls matte in error during newaza and the contestants separate because of the matte call, the referee and judges may, if possible, replace the contestants as close to their original positions as possible and restart the contest, in accordance with the majority of three rule, if doing so will rectify an injustice to one of the contestants.

After the announcement of matte, the contestants must quickly return to the position in which they started the contest. When the referee has announced matte, the contestants must either stand if being spoken to or adjusting their uniforms or sit if a lengthy delay is expected. Only when receiving medical attention should a contestant be permitted to adopt any other position.

The referee may announce matte if a contestant is injured or indisposed and may ask the contestant's accredited doctor to come into the competition area and proceed with a quick examination. The referee may announce matte if a contestant who is injured indicates to the referee that he requires an examination. This must be undertaken as quickly as possible. (See article 29.) The referee may announce matte if the Referee Commission, on the request of the accredited team doctor, authorizes the doctor to undertake a quick examination of an injured contestant. (See article 29.)

Declaration of Ippon

Article 20 covers when the referee can declare ippon. The referee will announce ippon when in his opinion an applied technique corresponds to the following criteria:

- When a contestant with control throws the other contestant largely on his back with considerable force and speed
- When a contestant holds the other contestant with osaekomiwaza and the held contestant is unable to get away for 25 seconds after the announcement of osaekomi
- When a contestant gives up by tapping twice or more with his hand or foot or says maitta, generally as a result of a grappling technique such as shimewaza or kansetsuwaza
- When a contestant is incapacitated by the effect of shimewaza or kansetsuwaza

If a contestant is penalized four shidos or one direct hansoku maka, the other contestant will be declared the winner.

Simultaneous ippon is covered in article 19 of the rules. When both contestants fall to the mat after what appear to be simultaneous attacks and the referee and judges cannot judge which technique dominated, no score is awarded. This is referred to as simultaneous technique.

During newaza, if the referee announces ippon in error and the contestants separate, the referee and judges may replace the contestants as close to their original positions as possible and restart the contest, if it can be done in accordance with the majority of three rule and if so doing will rectify an injustice to one of the contestants.

If one of the contestants deliberately makes a bridge (head and heels in contact with the mat) after being thrown, although he may have avoided the necessary criteria for ippon, the referee may nonetheless award ippon or any other score he considers that the technique warrants, to discourage this action.

Using kansetsuwaza to throw the opponent will not be considered for point-scoring purposes. Tori may use uke's attempt to avoid the armlock. For example, if uke tries to do a forward roll to get out of the armlock, tori can capitalize on the defensive maneuver and follow into newaza.

Note: For Olympic Games, world championships, continental events, and IJF events, the rule will be applied as stated. For national events, the organizers are authorized to make provisions as appropriate for the safety of the contestants at the level to which the tournament applies. For example, in lower-grade competition the organizers may authorize the referees to award ippon when the effect of a technique is sufficiently apparent. For children's events, the organizers may disallow shimewaza and kansetsuwaza altogether for safety reasons.

Article 21 covers wazari awasete ippon. If a contestant gains a second wazari in the contest (see article 23), the referee shall announce wazari awasete ippon.

Article 22 states that the referee will announce sogogachi (compound win) under the following conditions:

- A contestant gains a wazari and his opponent subsequently receives a penalty of three shidos (see article 27).

- A contestant, whose opponent has already received a penalty of three shidos, is subsequently awarded a wazari.

Article 19 describes simultaneous sogogachi.

Declaration of Wazari

Article 23 covers when a referee should announce wazari rather than ippon. The referee will announce wazari when in his opinion the applied technique corresponds to the following criteria:

- A contestant with control throws the other contestant, but the technique is partially lacking in one of the four elements necessary for ippon (see article 20).

- A contestant holds the other contestant with osaekomiwaza and the other contestant is unable to get away for 20 seconds.

If a contestant is penalized three shidos, the other contestant receives wazari immediately.

Although the criteria for ippon may be present—specifically, throwing from the back with speed and force as evident in a throw such as tomoe nage—if there is an interruption to the throw, wazari is the maximum score that should be awarded.

Declaration of Yuko

When a contestant with control throws the other contestant but the technique is partially lacking in two of the other three elements necessary for ippon, the referee will announce yuko (article 24). For example, yuko will apply if the technique is partially lacking in the element of largely on the back and is also partially lacking in either of the other two elements of speed and force. Yuko also applies if the technique is largely on the back but partially lacking in both the other two elements of speed and force. Yuko also is appropriate when a contestant holds the other contestant with osaekomiwaza, and the other contestant is unable to get away for 15 seconds.

If a contestant is penalized two shidos, the other contestant receives yuko immediately.

Regardless of how many yukos are announced, no amount will be considered equal to a wazari. The total number announced will be recorded.

Declaration of Koka

The referee announces koka when in his opinion the applied technique corresponds to the following criteria (article 25):

- A contestant with control throws the other contestant onto one shoulder, the thigh or thighs, or buttocks with speed and force.
- A contestant holds the other contestant with osaekomiwaza, and the other contestant is unable to get away for 10 seconds.

If a contestant is penalized one shido, the other contestant receives koka immediately.

Regardless of how many kokas are announced, no amount is considered equal to a yuko or wazari. The total number announced will be recorded.

Throwing an opponent on the front of his body, knees, hands, or elbows will be counted as the same as any other attack. Similarly, an osaekomi of up to 9 seconds will be counted as an attack.

Declaration of Osaekomiwaza

The referee announces osaekomi when in his opinion the applied technique meets the criteria (article 26). Osaekomi is announced when the contestant being held is controlled by his opponent and has his back and one or both shoulders in contact with the mat. The control can be made from the side, the rear, or the top. The contestant applying the hold must not have his legs or body controlled by his opponent's legs. At least one contestant must have a part of his body touching the contest area at the announcement of osaekomi. The contestant applying the hold must have his body in either the kesa or the shiho position, similar to the techniques kesa gatame and kamishiho gatame.

If a contestant who is controlling his opponent with an osaekomi changes without losing control into another osaekomi, the osaekomi time will continue until the announcement of ippon, wazari, the equivalent in the case of wazari awasete ippon, toketa, or matte.

If the contestant in the position of advantage commits a foul that merits a penalty while applying osaekomi, the referee announces matte, returns the contestants to their starting positions, awards the penalty and any score from the osaekomi, and then recommences the contest by announcing hajime.

If the contestant in the disadvantaged position commits a foul that merits a penalty while osaekomi is being applied, the referee announces sono mama, awards the penalty, and recommences the contest by touching both contestants and announcing yoshi. However, if the penalty awarded is hansoku maka, the referee acts in accordance with article 27.

If both judges agree that an osaekomi exists but the referee has not announced osaekomi, they should indicate it with the osaekomi signal, and, by the majority of three rule, the referee announces osaekomi immediately.

The referee announces matte in the case of osaekomi on the edge, when the one part of the contestant still touching the contest area loses contact with the mat.

Toketa is announced if, during osaekomi, the contestant being held succeeds in scissoring the other contestant's leg, either from above or below the leg.

During newaza, if after the announcement of sono mama the penalty to be given is hansoku maka, matte should be announced, hansoku maka awarded, and the contest ended with soremade.

If uke's back is no longer in contact with the mat (bridging) but tori maintains control, the osaekomi shall continue.

Prohibited Acts and Penalties

Prohibited acts are divided into slight infringements (shido) and grave infringements (hansoku maka). The referee awards a penalty of shido or hansoku maka depending on the seriousness of the infringement.

The awarding of a second or subsequent shido automatically reflects on the opponent's technical score. The previous score corresponding to the earlier penalty is removed and the next higher score is recorded immediately.

The awarding of a direct hansoku maka means the contestant is disqualified and excluded from the tournament. The contest ends according to article 19.

A referee awarding a penalty should demonstrate with a simple action the reason for the penalty.

A penalty can be awarded after the announcement of soremade for any prohibited act committed during the time allotted for the contest or, in some exceptional situations, for serious acts committed after the signal to end the contest, as long as the decision has not been given.

Shido

Shido is given to any contestant who has committed a slight infringement, such as negative judo, invalid gripping, or noncombativity.

Negative judo is legal as long as the judoka stays within the guidelines of the rules. Negative judo is defined as follows:

- Intentionally avoiding taking hold to prevent action in the contest
- Adopting an excessively defensive posture (generally for more than 5 seconds) while standing
- Giving the impression of an attack without an intent to throw the opponent (false attack)
- Standing with both feet completely in the danger zone (generally for more than 5 seconds) unless beginning an attack, executing an attack, countering the opponent's attack, or defending against the opponent's attack
- While standing, continuously holding the end of the opponent's sleeve for a defensive purpose (generally more than 5 seconds) or grasping by screwing up the sleeve
- While standing, continuously keeping the opponent's fingers of one or both hands interlocked (generally more than 5 seconds) to prevent action in the contest
- Intentionally disarranging one's own judogi or untying or retying the belt or the trousers without the referee's permission
- Pulling the opponent down to start newaza unless in accordance with article 16
- Inserting a finger or fingers inside the opponent's sleeve or the bottom of his trousers or grasping by screwing up his sleeve

In general, normal gripping means holding with the left hand any part of the right side of the opponent's jacket above the belt or holding with the right hand any part of the left side of the opponent's jacket above the belt. In a standing position, an invalid grip is any grip other than a normal grip that is taken without attacking, generally within 3 to 5 seconds.

Noncombativity results in shido being awarded to the opponent. Noncombativity is defined as not making any attacking moves while in a standing position after kumi kata has been established. Noncombativity may be assumed when, in general, for approximately 25 seconds, there have been no attacking actions on the part of either or both contestants. Noncombativity should not be awarded when there are no attacking actions if the referee considers that the contestant is genuinely looking for the opportunity to attack.

Miscellaneous minor infractions, such as the following, can also result in shido being awarded:

- From a standing position, taking hold of the opponent's foot or feet, legs, or trouser legs with the hands, unless simultaneously attempting a throwing technique
- Encircling the end of the belt or jacket around any part of the opponent's body
- Taking the judogi in the mouth
- Putting a hand, arm, foot, or leg directly on the opponent's face
- Putting a foot or leg in the opponent's belt, collar, or lapel

The act of encircling means that the belt or jacket must completely encircle. Using the belt or jacket as an anchor for a grip without encircling to, say, trap the opponent's arm should not be penalized.

When one contestant pulls his opponent down into newaza in a way that is not in accordance with article 16 and his opponent does not take advantage of this to continue into newaza, the referee announces matte, temporarily stops the contest, and awards shido to the contestant who has infringed article 16.

Hansoku Maka

Hansoku maka is awarded to any contestant who has committed a grave infringement or who commits a subsequent slight infringement after having been given three shidos. The following events will result in the awarding of hansoku maka to the opponent:

- Applying kawazugake—throwing the opponent by winding one leg around the opponent's leg while facing more or less in the same direction as the opponent and falling backward onto him
- Applying kansetsuwake anywhere other than to the elbow joint
- Lifting an opponent who is lying on the tatami off the tatami and driving him back onto the tatami
- Reaping the opponent's supporting leg from the inside when the opponent is applying a technique such as haraigoshi
- Disregarding the referee's instructions
- Making unnecessary derogatory calls, remarks, or gestures to the opponent or referee during the contest
- Taking any action that may endanger or injure the opponent, especially the opponent's neck or spinal vertebrae, or may be against the spirit of judo

- Falling directly to the mat while applying or attempting to apply techniques such as wakigatame
- Diving headfirst onto the mat by bending forward and downward while performing or attempting to perform techniques such as uchimata or haraigoshi
- Falling directly backward while performing or attempting to perform techniques such as kataguruma while standing or kneeling
- Intentionally falling backward when the other contestant is clinging to your back and when either contestant has control of the other's movement
- Wearing a hard or metallic object, covered or not

On the scoreboard, the repeated shido will be accumulated and converted to the opponent's technical score. Two shidos would result in a yuko to the opponent. Three shidos results in a wazari to the opponent. Four shidos equal a hansoku maka and ippon for the opponent.

Before awarding hansoku maka, the referee must consult with the judges and make his decision in accordance with the majority of three rule. When both contestants infringe the rules at the same time, each should be awarded a penalty according to the degree of the infringement. When both contestants have been awarded three shidos and subsequently each receives a further penalty, they should both be declared hansoku maka. Nonetheless, the officials may make their final decision in this matter in accordance with article 30.

Three shidos or hansoku maka in newaza should be applied in the same manner as in osaekomi (article 26).

RULE CHANGES

Although the rules change, the intent of the rules has remained the same over a number of years. The technical aspects as opposed to the intent are in constant refinement and transition.

Astute competitors stay aware as rules are changed and interpreted. But as I worked through this book, I realized that the intent of the rules can be used as a guideline for all aspects of judo, from techniques to tactics to the use of appropriate drills. To effectively pass through the gateways of judo, drills and simulations must be designed to fit within the boundaries of the rules. Effective fighters become proactive by designing strategies that use these rule changes to their advantage.

Your intent throughout the match must be to attempt positive judo. Positive judo means attempting to score on your opponent. Although the best efforts of the IJF continue to make judo more dynamic and spectator friendly, astute competitors have found ways to manipulate the match so that the opponent receives penalties. This is known as negative judo and is perfectly legal as long as the judoka acts within the guideline of the rules. (See article 27 for more on negative judo.)

The following rule changes have profoundly affected sport judo:

- **Penalties**. Originally penalties were imposed to outlaw actions such as biting and gouging because of safety concerns. Recent changes were introduced to make judo a spectator-friendly sport, although the changes became a double-edged sword as competitors learned to manipulate the rules. A judoka must know both how to avoid and how to impose the threat of penalties as seen in the passive penalty and false attack penalty.

- **New gripping rules**. To eliminate defensive gripping, IJF rules outlaw holding any unorthodox grip for more than 3 seconds. Nevertheless, a judoka needs to study unorthodox grips. Although they are held only briefly, they are part of the setup for throws such as kata guruma drop seoi nage and one-sided uchimata.

- **Introduction of the golden score (sudden death overtime)**. The sudden death overtime is the most significant change in 30 years because it has almost eliminated the referee's need to make tie-breaking decisions. If the score is tied at the end of the 5-minute regulation time, the score is reset to zero and the clock is reset for another 5 minutes. The first judoka to receive a score or impose a penalty on his opponent wins the match. If neither judoka scores during the 5 minutes of overtime, the referee and corner judges determine the winner. This rule change has had a major influence on both tactics and conditioning.

Since the inclusion of the golden score, only rarely have the officials had to determine a winner. Judoka are more intent on scoring rather than just wasting energy trying to impress the officials in order to win the decision. Fighters are more focused on scoring in order to avoid having to go into overtime. A judoka must be fit enough to last up to 10 minutes in a fight instead of only five minutes. Chapters 7 and 8 cover the elements of drills and conditioning so you can use this rule to your advantage.

Now that you have a general understanding of the rules, let's get into the first topic for competitive judo: offensive and defensive body positions.

2

Offensive and Defensive Body Positioning

The first goal in preparing for a competition is to anticipate success. This might not be a whole-hearted belief that you will win, though that would obviously be best. Instead it might be a belief that you can achieve a small victory over your opponent such as obtaining a specific grip that in turn will allow you to set up your attack, giving you a good chance to apply a technique that affords you a chance to score and thus a chance to win.

When you are fighting a strong opponent, it is often easier to break down the fight into small segments, or gates, and work through each gateway until matte is called. It is imperative that you concentrate on the stage, or gate, of the action that you are performing at any given moment. This is often referred to as *staying in the moment*. Some judoka do this naturally, and some must train to achieve this state, but all champions must have controlled concentration and focus. Throughout this book I identify each gateway, or step, of the scrimmage; in fact, the book is written in the order of the task of each gateway. You will find it counterproductive to worry about the gateways you recently passed through or the gateways yet to come.

Remember that the more nervous you are before the fight, the more you will need a good warm-up. Nervousness is your mind preparing your body to do something very special.

From the beginning of the fight, you must go after your grip. You must not settle for anything less than a sound grip. This is the small task, but when you secure the grip or situation, you will have a number of appropriate setups to use. You can then use the attacks you have trained to execute automatically after hours of drilling. After your attack, follow up with the transition into groundwork using the most efficient path to the groundwork technique you will apply. Only at the call of matte or ippon does the action stop.

At the referee's call of matte, force yourself to breathe as you have been trained—two short, sharp inhales through the nose and one hard exhale out the mouth to gain control over your breathing. This will help to compensate for the oxygen debt, to reevaluate the situation, and to refocus, concentrating again and again on controlling your grip. Start the whole process over again, as many times as is necessary to win.

Time analyses indicate that judo matches usually consist of 10 30-second scrimmages in a 5-minute bout with 10 15- to 20-second rest phases. It is better to plan to go for the whole 5 minutes so as to prepare yourself for a hard, grueling match, rather than to visualize a glorious match-stopping move early in the fight. Remember, you go onto the mat to work, not to be glorious.

After winning a match, walk around or do light aerobic exercise to burn off the accumulated lactic acid. Then relax and bring yourself down to a gentle state of recovery; the natural excitement of the day will bring you back up to the arousal level you will need for the next fight. If you stay in a highly excited state all day, you will be exhausted in the later rounds of the competition.

Of course, every fight is unique, but this general plan has worked well for me and many of my students. As you can see, all scrimmages start with the grip because it is the initial control setup for the entire scrimmage.

GRIPS

Judo has been compared to physical chess, and gripping is the first tactical and technical step in the game. By using various gripping situations and body positions, a judoka can gain control and advantage over the opponent. This chapter covers a number of different grips and demonstrates the ways of obtaining the preferred grip.

There are two main gripping categories: ayotsu, in which both fighters grip right or left; and kenkayotsu, in which opponents hold opposing grips with right against left or left against right. Both categories have their advantages and disadvantages covered later in this chapter.

Five Golden Rules of Gripping

The five golden rules outlined in this section fit all gripping situations at all level of competition. The more often you break these rules, the more chances your opponent has on which to capitalize!

First, when gripping your opponent, grip with only the bottom three fingers. Tuck the two top fingers out of the way (figure 2.1). This significantly eliminates the buildup of fatigue and lactic acid in the forearm by using the main muscles of the wrist and forearm and avoiding the use of some smaller muscles that fatigue more quickly.

Second, when attempting to secure a high collar grip, do not lunge toward uke. Lunging will present a good opportunity for uke to use your momentum to attack you. To secure a collar grip, it is much safer to secure uke's sleeve (or preferably the lapel) and use the strong twisting action of your

Figure 2.1   Grip with the bottom three fingers and tuck the top two fingers out of the way.

shoulders to bring uke's shoulders to you.

Third, when gripping, avoid reaching above your shoulder height. If you are fighting someone taller than you, bring uke's shoulders down to your height or use a grip that doesn't require you to reach up, such as a double lapel or sleeve lapel grip. To lower uke's shoulders, it is best to rotate uke's shoulders down as opposed to trying to bend uke at the waist.

Fourth, never have straight arms while reaching for or after securing a collar or lapel grip. Straight arms make you susceptible to front dropping throws such as drop seoi nage or drop kata guruma as well as to standing armlocks. Always have a slight bend in your elbow because this ensures that your shoulders are relaxed and puts the weight of your body onto your opponent.

Finally, when you get your grip, your opponent must feel as though a rope is stretched across his shoulders. Observers should actually see a directed line of tension in uke's judogi form between tori's two hands (figure 2.2).

Figure 2.2   Grip tightly to exercise maximum control over uke.

The more directed the line, the more control tori has over uke. Adjust your hand positioning on uke's sleeve, collar, or lapel to create the most direct line to achieve maximum control over uke.

When moving with your grip in place, never allow your thumbs to move behind your own shoulders or you will surrender control of the grip to uke.

Sleeve Lapel Grip

The sleeve lapel grip is the first grip introduced to most judoka. It is a fairly neutral grip, giving neither opponent much of an advantage. The real value to this grip is for training. Because a judoka will not physically dominate an opponent with this grip, it forces a judoka to use timing, speed, and technique to throw the opponent.

When I was a junior training at my sensei's dojo, we were allowed to use only the sleeve lapel grip, and that helped us greatly in learning good principles of judo. When guests would come, they too were encouraged to use only the sleeve lapel grip. If they chose not to, my sensei believed it was a good opportunity for us to train to exploit the weaknesses and understand the strengths of the other gripping styles. Fighting under these gripping restrictions certainly made us aware of the importance of a dominant grip.

Usually for the sleeve lapel grip, tori holds the sleeve between uke's elbow and wrist with the left hand (figure 2.3). Tori's right hand then holds the opponent's lapel at approximately midchest level of the judogi. With this grip, tori may execute most types of throws and perform them on either the right or left side. But this versatility comes with a price—the opponent has the same

Figure 2.3   Sleeve lapel grip.

opportunities and versatility. This situation is excellent for developing judo but is completely unacceptable in competition. Even the amazingly skillful Yamashita preaches that you must control the grips in competition.

> **Fine point:** While holding the sleeve lapel grip, bend your elbow; when your elbows are bent, uke must carry your weight around his neck while you can rest your arms and use your body weight to hold your opponent under your control.

The most common error is to hold every opponent by the lapels at the same height for all throws. You must adjust your hand position for different throws as you place your hands on both the sleeve and the lapel. With lifting throws, use a higher lapel hand position along with a lower sleeve grip. But rotating or dropping throws call for lower lapel hand positioning.

Sleeve Collar Grip

The sleeve collar grip is the grip most commonly used in competition. Once a judoka obtains this grip over uke, it is relatively easy for tori to pull uke's weight forward. Thus, to maintain his own balance, uke must retract his hips, putting himself in a poor attacking position. If uke remains too bent over, he could be penalized for standing in a defensive position. One other strength of this grip is that it can be used in either an ayotsu or a kenkayotsu situation. The collar lapel grip enables you to attack strongly with lifting throws such as uchimata and hip techniques, and reasonably well with rotating throws such as taiotoshi, haraigoshi, and sasae ashi, mentioned under the double lapel grip. By simply dropping your elbow and making contact with uke's upper chest, you can use that contact to help you rotate uke's shoulders. If this fails to produce sufficient rotation, fighters often simply let go of the collar in the final stages of a rotating throw, wind themselves around the opponent, and finish off in a makikomi style throw.

There is a limitation to the sleeve collar grip: It is very difficult to attack to the collar side of your opponent with major throws without rearranging the grip. If you choose to use the sleeve collar grip, you must be aware that it is a strong grip once attained; if you are trying to secure the collar improperly, you are giving your opponent an opportunity to attack with a throw or standing armlock.

With the sleeve collar grip, tori secures a sleeve and collar grip. In an ayotsu situation, tori has the freedom to hold the sleeve from midforearm to elbow height (figure 2.4), but in a kenkayotsu approach, to ensure control of the opponent's shoulder as well as the sleeve, tori must grab from between the elbow and midbiceps (figure 2.5). To secure the collar, tori should grip beside the neck with the wrist and elbow bent so that tori's forearm rests along uke's upper chest.

Figure 2.4 Sleeve collar grip in ayotsu situation; tori holds sleeve between uke's midforearm and elbow; uke controls tori's shoulder by holding his lapel.

Figure 2.5 Sleeve collar grip in kenkayotsu situation; tori holds sleeve between uke's elbow and midbiceps; uke holds tori's sleeve.

Fine points

1. Secure the sleeve first. Once you have secured the sleeve, slightly rotate your body and pull your opponent's sleeve down toward your right hip.

2. Only when you can see the top of your opponent's head do you attempt to grab your opponent's collar. This ensures that your opponent's head is down and that you are not reaching above your shoulders with your right hand while getting your grip.

3. Always maintain a slight bend in your elbow.

A common error with the sleeve collar grip is when tori allows the collar hand to drift behind his own shoulder, thus offering a good chance for uke to attack or counter tori's attempted throw.

Double Lapel Grip

The double lapel grip is an extremely powerful grip that gives tori control over both of uke's shoulders, making it difficult for uke to apply a meaningful attack. Obviously, uke will not like this feeling of being controlled and will let go of the grip to improve his position. In this moment, tori must attack his opponent because, with only one hand on tori, it is difficult for uke to defend or counter tori's attack.

The double lapel grip is best done in an ayotsu situation (same-side stance). In the case of a right to right stance, tori grips the gi at the opponent's armpit on the left side (figure 2.6). It is preferred that tori grip over uke's arm and that tori rest his forearm on uke's forearm. Tori can apply pressure down on uke's left arm by rotating his left wrist downward, thus obtaining control of uke's left shoul-

Figure 2.6 Double lapel grip.

der. Note that it is vitally important that tori does not apply the downward pressure from anything other than the wrist or tori's shoulder will drop, neutralizing tori's control over uke's shoulder and limiting tori's ability to move freely. Tori's right hand grabs uke's right lapel anywhere between uke's chest and neck, depending on the situation.

The recommended throws with this grip are throws that rotate uke's shoulders to create kezushi (off-balancing). Such throws would be taiotoshi, haraigoshi, seoi nage, sasae ashi, leg picks, kata guruma, and hizaguruma. Many of these throws can be applied to the right or left side.

For the double lapel grip, the main concern is for tori to control uke's shoulders. This control limits uke's ability to rotate his shoulder and prevents uke from applying a meaningful attack. On a right-handed fighter, tori would circle toward uke's left shoulder and apply a cross grip to feed uke's lapel toward tori's left hand. This must be done very rapidly. Once tori grips uke's armpit, tori pulls his left elbow toward his hip, putting uke's weight on uke's left leg. As tori's left elbow pulls in, tori's right hand grabs uke's right lapel or collar.

Uke will make one of two likely reactions. If tori holds the cross grip too long, uke may grab tori's right wrist. This is an inconvenience, but because uke's arm is outstretched, it should be relatively easy for tori to free his hand and continue on with the grip. Second, uke may try to regrip with his right hand to either tori's lapel or collar. This action provides tori with a good attacking opportunity.

The weakness of the double lapel grip arises in a kenkayotsu situation (right versus left or vice versa). For a right-handed fighter to grip the left lapel of a left-handed opponent, tori would have to break one of the golden rules of gripping and reach out and grab with a straight arm. Doing this would put all of tori's balance on his left foot. This combined with the lack of control of uke's shoulders puts tori in a vulnerable position. A left-handed uke would simply grab the end of tori's sleeve on the outstretched arm and clamp it to his body. Uke would then control tori.

Figure 2.7 Hold uke's lower lapel and rotate your hand so that your palm is turned upward.

The remedy kenkayotsu is to control uke's right shoulder with your right grip and then grab uke's lapel low, just above uke's belt, and bring your elbow into your hip, thus controlling uke's left hip (figure 2.7). Should uke grab the end of your left sleeve, you have the choice of maintaining that grip or snatching the end of uke's sleeve so that it is taut. That places uke in an undesirable position.

Fine point: While holding uke's lower lapel in a kenkayotsu situation, rotate your hand so that your palm is turned upward.

The name *double lapel grip* is a little misleading. It is more accurate to call it an armpit lapel grip, but I will stick to tradition and use the more common name. For a right-handed grip on a right-handed opponent (ayotsu situation), grab uke's left armpit or outer chest area. With your left hand, grab uke's right lapel. Your right hand must be over uke's collar grip, which is his left arm. In a left versus right situation (kenkayotsu), it is more common to grab both lapels.

The double lapel grip has a couple of advantages. First, you will have excellent control over your opponent's shoulders, restricting uke's ability to rotate into a throw. Second, with this control over uke's shoulders, not only can you apply rotating throws such as taiotoshi, shoulder throws, kata guruma, leg grabs, and many ashiwaza, but you can also apply many of these techniques right or left.

The disadvantages of the double lapel grip are that it is difficult to apply lifting throws such as uchimata, and you must always fight to stay over your opponent's arm as he grabs your collar. This can become tiring.

Do not allow uke to gain control over your shoulders by reaching over your arm and grabbing your collar. Also avoid walking straight back or diagonally to the rear instead of in a circling manner.

Fine points for fighting ayotsu

1. When you move in a circling manner, do so in the direction in which you are controlling uke's shoulder.

2. At all times, keep your lead foot outside uke's foot.

3. When applying pressure on uke's arm, do so with movement from the wrist. Be sure not to lower your own shoulder.

4. The control over uke's shoulder must be reminiscent of a bullfighter's use of his cape. Bring your opponent's shoulder just past your own shoulder. This gives you much more control.

Unorthodox Grips

The inclusion of the Soviet Union in international judo competition brought some major changes in style. The Eastern Bloc judoka had a much more bent over, wrestling posture. In the old Soviet Union and to this day in Russia, Russians practice a sport called sombo, an interesting mix of judo and wrestling. Sombo combatants wear what resembles a tight judo top, a cloth belt, and shorts. Because gripping restrictions in sombo are almost nonexistent, this freedom has fostered some very interesting gripping strategies.

Perhaps as a result of Eastern Bloc influences, the IJF changed some rules regarding gripping, including adding this rule: Defensive or unorthodox grips may be held for only 3 to 5 seconds before the judoka attacks or releases the grip without receiving a penalty. This ruling has not changed for a number of years, but what are considered unorthodox grips do change periodically.

The following sections in no way cover all of the unorthodox grips, but they do cover the main ones used in judo competition today.

Cross Grip

In the cross grip, your hand crosses your own body to grab your opponent's gi (figure 2.8). This grip can be used to set up a throw as with eri taiotoshi or the kouchigari leg grab finish, as well as with different versions of the leg grab. Or it can be used to feed your opponent's gi to your other hand to set up gripping patterns.

Figure 2.8   Cross grip.

> **Fine point:** With a cross grip it is vital that you pull inward toward your own body so as to maintain control over uke's shoulders. Your hand must be in constant motion during this grip to keep uke unsettled.

The most common mistake is to hold on to the cross grip too long. Not only does this carry the risk of penalty, but by holding the cross grip too long or too statically, you give your opponent a chance to gain control over your wrist and apply a sleeve back grip to neutralize your control.

Under current rules, tori is allowed to hold this grip for only 3 seconds before putting in an attack or a shido penalty is applied.

Sleeve Back Grip

For a sleeve back grip, a right-handed fighter grabs the opponent's sleeve with the left hand and reaches over the opponent's back with his right hand to grab across the opponent's back in a variety of places (figure 2.9). This technique is an excellent defensive grip because it gives the fighter good control over the opponent's shoulder. In addition, experts in the use of this grip have developed a number of effective attacks from this position: leg grabs, various ashiwaza, kata guruma, sustemi waza, and often a one-sided uchimata, used either to score or to set up other throws.

> **Fine point:** You must have a strong inward and downward pull on uke's sleeve to control uke's shoulder. It is often possible to rest your body weight on uke's arm to add extra control.

The sleeve back grip is most powerful when you don't allow uke to hold on to your gi, but occasionally it is impossible to remove uke's grip on your collar. You must clamp uke's wrist to your chest and slightly rotate your body to gain control over uke's shoulder before you grab his back.

Figure 2.9 Sleeve back grip.

One-Handed Fighting

In one-handed fighting, tori secures a lapel grip and fights off the opponent's attempt to get the second grip (figure 2.10). This is done mostly to use or frustrate uke's attempt to secure the second hand grip on tori. Uke opens himself up so tori can deliver a sound attack. Seoi nage specialists and judoka who use a lot of leg picks often use this grip. A less common one-handed grip, but one that is very effective, is for tori to hold on to the sleeve so as to set up uke for a throw.

A common error is for tori to hold with a stiff arm, giving the impression of a defensive position. Tori must keep his wrist, elbow, and shoulder loose and constantly hunt for an opportunity to attack.

Figure 2.10 One-handed fighting.

Fine point: Tori should use an effective small fanning action with his gripping arm to parry uke's attempts to get a grip.

Fighting Kenkayotsu Sleeve Collar Grip

Before reading about the fighting kenkayotsu sleeve collar grip, familiarize yourself with the sleeve collar grip and its strengths and limitations (see page 25). This grip is for a kenkayotsu situation in which tori is right and uke is left (figure 2.11).

As tori steps out toward uke, tori starts to shift slightly to uke's right side from which uke attempts to grab tori's lapel or collar. As tori moves closer to uke, tori suddenly rotates his shoulders to his right and away from uke's left (or power) hand. This rotation keeps tori's right shoulder at arm's reach from uke. This is all done when tori and uke are a few inches back from arm's length of each other.

Figure 2.11   Fighting kenkayotsu collar sleeve grip.

(Body position and spatial awareness are learned skills and must be part of the learning process when studying gripping. There is a more complete discussion on circling and spatial awareness in the section on circling, beginning on page 85.)

When obtaining a grip in a kenkayotsu situation, tori often uses a cross grip to momentarily control uke's shoulder, enabling tori to secure a sound grip with tori's opposite hand on uke's targeted side. The major problem with using a cross grip against an experienced fighter is that you may sacrifice your sleeve to your opponent, which could be a major disadvantage unless you are well prepared.

There are two tactics to be aware of when applying a cross grip. First, fighters who are new to cross gripping often apply the grip too slowly and hold it too long. This gives the opponent time to secure a good grip on tori's sleeve, which is a huge disadvantage for tori. Remember, the basic cross grip is used to control uke's shoulder momentarily while making a handle out of uke's gi and making it easier for tori to grab the targeted area on uke's gi.

The cross grip must be applied with the speed of a boxer's jab; the second hand follows up with equal velocity. You will know if you have done it quickly enough if your opponent's head momentarily bobs down, then up. This bobbing action is induced not by strength but by speed and body movement. (This type of hand speed is referred to as *absolute speed*; it is discussed in the chapter on conditioning, page 157.)

Second, after tori pulls out the lapel of uke's gi with the left hand, tori grabs the collar or lapel with the right hand. Hopefully, tori is fast enough to retract his left hand before uke gains control over tori's sleeve. If not, tori can free the sleeve with a snapping action to the left (see page 37 for a more detailed explanation).

At this point tori has two options:

1. Tori can attack with a one-handed grip to uke's right front shoulder by applying any one-handed attack such as kata guruma or seoi nage.

2. Tori can grab again with the left hand on uke's lapel and apply an eri taiotoshi or a makikomi movement.

To apply either of these throws, tori must retract his left foot and pull with the left hand, momentarily putting herself in a right stance. Tori would then attack with one of the mentioned throws in a normal fashion. Tori then follows up into groundwork in the most efficient manner.

Tori also has the option of securing the sleeve as he applies the sleeve collar grip. This may be done if uke does not grab tori's sleeve or if tori grabs the high part of uke's right lapel, keeping the left arm bent and close to his own body while maintaining the grip with his right hand. Tori now has an opportunity to make a second attack such as taiotoshi, uchimata, or haraigoshi, all to tori's right corner, or tori might choose to use ouchigari or kouchigari to tori's right back corner or to let go of the opponent's left lapel and apply the technique. Without control over uke's left shoulder, tori must use his left forearm to unbalance uke as tori's left hand stays static. As tori's left arm keeps contact with uke's chest, tori rotates his shoulders and, through the contact of his own right arm, breaks uke's balance by twisting uke's shoulders one way as uke's feet point another way. At this point, tori has secured control and can attack with any of the throws.

Tori grabs the second lapel of uke's gi and then reaches around uke's forearm to grab above uke's elbow and obtain control over uke's right shoulder. With this control over uke's right shoulder, tori needs to rely much less on his right hand for unbalancing uke. Tori is better off pulling uke's right shoulder in so as to rotate uke's shoulders. Once uke is unbalanced, tori is free to attack with one of the throws.

Fine point: Tori must reach over uke's forearm to put uke's arm on the inside to secure more control over uke's arm and shoulder.

Grip Fighting

It is important to study the art of gripping to increase your chances of scoring either with a throw or by winning a penalty. Getting your grip—or grip fighting (figure 2.12), as it is commonly called—is as varied and sophisticated as any aspect of judo.

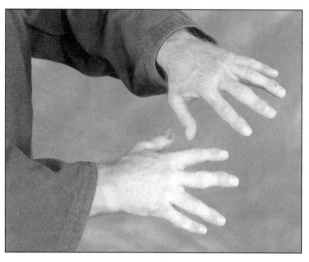

Figure 2.12   Hands after 30 years of grip fighting.

In my training, I was not introduced to the subtlety of gripping until I moved to Britain, where I trained with British fighter Dave Starbrook, famous for his great strength and superb conditioning. Dave won a medal in every European and World Championship, all over a 6-year period, as well as in two consecutive Olympic Games. When I first arrived in Britain, I found it very difficult to keep up with the fast pace of British judo. I was very young and trying to match the top British player's advanced gripping was very challenging because I had been trained strictly in the sleeve and lapel grips. Using this neutral grip with judoka who had equal or better judo skills than myself was not a great strategy. I was repeatedly outgripped and felt constantly one step behind my opponent. Naturally, Dave recognized this shortcoming in my judo and introduced me to a number of different grips and gripping strategies he had used very effectively in international competitions.

Now that I have covered the actual grips, as well as their advantages and disadvantages, I will review how to get the grips in the heat of a contest.

The most efficient way to train for grip fighting is to drill by repeating set patterns of hand and foot movements while having your training partner move and react as he would in competition, though at a much slower speed. You can realistically predict that your opponent will respond with one or two reactions.

To be a great grip fighter, you must begin your planned strategy well before you lay a hand on your opponent. You must decide which side of your opponent you walk out to, the direction in which you circle, the angle at which you hold your shoulders, and which hand you grab with first. All of these factors affect the outcome of the battle for the grips, and ultimately how or whether you obtain control over your opponent. This all comes with time and practice as with any skill. (Efficient drills save time!)

First, tori goes through the patterns slowly. Once tori is comfortable with the pattern, training partners increase the speed and the resistance of their movements. Eventually, the stepping patterns and hand movements become automatic. Once tori gets to this point, it is time to try the whole gripping pattern on lower-ranked opponents.

A word of warning: Do not pick an opponent of too low a caliber; his reactions may be too slow or just inappropriate, and thus throw your own pattern off. Once you start achieving success with lower-ranked players, slowly move up the ranks to more challenging opponents.

The more automatic your gripping patterns are, the more effective they will be at keeping you one step ahead of your opponent. Remember, if you're controlling your opponent by obtaining your grip first, your next move is to throw uke. But uke's next move is to neutralize your grip so that uke can attempt a meaningful attack by either scoring with a counter or by winning a penalty.

Gaining and maintaining a controlling grip is a huge advantage. It gives you an excellent chance to set up your throw. It puts uke under the pressure of neutralizing your grip, or of attacking from a weak position and risking a counter or a penalty for false attack if uke's attack fails to meet the criteria. If uke simply goes into a defensive position to hold off your attack, then uke will risk a penalty.

Grip fighting means both neutralizing your opponent's grips and removing your opponent's grips.

Neutralizing Uke's Grip

No matter how good your gripping is, at some point everyone gets into a bad situation and wants to break free from the control of the opponent's grip. You must be aware of these key elements of your opponent's grip.

If your opponent is controlling the shoulder of your pulling hand, it would be best not to attack with any sort of forward throw such as taiotoshi or seoi nage. You can, however, still apply throws that drive into uke such as ouchigari, kouchigari, and leg picks. But before you attack under such conditions, create some freedom of movement for your shoulders by dropping your controlled shoulder down and out (figure 2.13). Only when you feel the release of control over your shoulder should you apply the technique.

Figure 2.13   Free your shoulders by dropping the controlled shoulder down and out.

In the obviously unacceptable situation of uke's controlling your sleeve, you must immediately neutralize uke's control by grabbing his wrist and drawing your elbow into your hip while you simultaneously twist uke's wrist upside down (figure 2.14). This is surprisingly easy because uke has nothing to brace against while holding on to just the sleeve of your gi. Nevertheless, this solution is admittedly somewhat of a standoff. Neither you nor uke has good enough control over the other's pulling arm to administer a particularly strong attack. Most often uke will find it unnerving to have his wrist twisted and arm outstretched and will let go of your sleeve and retract his arm. Of course you will have little chance to stop uke's action because holding on to just the bare wrist gives you no real control. But if you drill for uke's reaction of withdrawing his arm, then uke's action affords you a good opportunity to step in with a strong attack of your own.

Figure 2.14   Neutralize uke's control of your sleeve.

In reaction to uke's controlling your sleeve, simply retract your elbow slightly to cause a slight strain on uke's grip and the end of your sleeve. The instant you feel the strain on the end of your sleeve, bring your hand up and over uke's wrist. Your hand action should come mostly from your own wrist. Immediately after your hand crosses uke's wrist, forcefully drive your hand down between uke's body and your own body and attack with seoi nage or kouchigari.

Removing Uke's Grip

Before discussing the removal or tearing away of uke's grip, let's cover some basics. The better your posture is while tearing off uke's grip, the less chance he has to throw you during your attempt to remove the grip. Always isolate uke's hand from the rest of his body by pressing up or down (depending on the situation) with your forearm on his forearm, or isolate his wrist by cross gripping and grabbing the end of the sleeve of his gripping hand.

The actual act of ripping off uke's grip is a two-step process:

1. After securing a grip near the end of uke's sleeve, create tension by rotating your wrist downward (figure 2.15a).

2. Once you feel that tension, straighten your back in a short, fast snapping move to create a second and stronger force to rip off uke's grip (figure 2.15b). It is vital that the sudden stiffening action of the back not be such a big movement that it throws you off balance.

3. Tori then retracts elbow controlling ukes sleeve.

a   b

Figure 2.15   Breaking uke's grip: *(a)* rotate wrist to create tension; *(b)* execute a short, fast snapping move to rip off uke's grip.

If the initial attempt to remove uke's grip fails (which often happens), simply maintain the tension on uke's wrist and immediately try again to snap off the grip in the same manner. You often will find the grip comes off much more easily the second time because you will catch uke instinctively trying to recover his grip. You can catch him with little or no hand contact on your gi.

If uke is controlling your sleeve, he has a good opportunity to attack you. You must take immediate action. With your free hand, take a cross grip on uke's sleeve, the sleeve of the hand with which uke is holding on to your sleeve. Create tension by rotating down the wrist of the hand with which you are cross gripping and by tucking your elbow and as much as possible of the forearm of the controlled arm into your body. Simultaneously straighten your back and push down with the hand that you are using to apply the cross grip. If you are unsuccessful in removing uke's grip, simply retry immediately.

The second option for escape is a bit unusual but very effective. If uke has your sleeve, secure a good grip on uke's collar with your free hand. With the other hand, the one uke is holding on to, reach back and grab the back of your own judo pants at your hamstring (figure 2.16). Create tension by pushing on uke's chest with your collar grip and rotating the wrist of the hand that is

Figure 2.16   Alternative method of escape.

holding on to your trousers. Once you create tension, straighten your leg in a fast snapping movement.

Uke's holding your lapel is in no way as dangerous a position as his controlling the end of your sleeve or controlling your shoulder with a high collar grip. But you may want to increase your position by obtaining a more dominant grip.

Removing an opponent's lapel grip is more a matter of timing than grip power. Again, the skill is a two-step process:

1. Create tension on your opponent's grip by grabbing the end of his sleeve and rotating your wrist downward.

2. Once you feel tension, make a small but fast action to straighten your back. If this move is insufficient to release the grip, simply try again.

Fine point: Slide your opponent's hand down and then off your lapel.

3

Throws and Throw Counters

The contribution of each national culture to sport judo is both invigorating and exciting. As a coach over the last 10 years, I have come to appreciate the cultural differences in judo and how they coincide with the cultural differences of various societies. Of course this is a very broad generalization but it interesting to note how the different styles of judo correspond to a judoka's culture. The Japanese, famous for their long hard workdays outside judo, use a similar training and fighting method with long hard practice in the dojo and try to fit as much judo into their training day as possible. As a spectator one must be impressed with the sheer volume of fine high-quality judo that the top Japanese competitors can fit into a 5-minute fight.

In contrast, the top Russian fighters seem much more systematic in their choice of training methods, with much more scientific analysis involving needs of the sport of judo, constantly testing lactic acid levels, experimenting, varying, probing, and borrowing skills and training methods from other sports such as sombo and wrestling. This fact too is reflected in the control, the methodical and efficient way in which a typical Russian judoka is customarily perceived to fight.

I greatly enjoy watching a top Russian fighter systematically control his opponent with a well-rehearsed series of grips and attacks. In contrast, the Japanese judoka practice randori for 3 hours a day, and I have known some who spend 7 hours a day in randori. Thus the Japanese gripping and throwing techniques are developed rhythmically and the Russians, who tend not to have the same level of throwing skills, approach the Japanese style tactically, controlling grips by blocking which in turn disrupts their opponents' judo and allows the Russian judoka to attack.

Of course this represents the two extremes of style and most countries combine elements of these two styles, but it interesting to note that the countries that have most contact with either extreme seem to lean more to that style of training.

On my first trip to Japan I had the great pleasure to visit Mr. Okono's dojo, Sykajuku. Mr. Okono is a former world Olympic and all-Japan champion and was gracious enough to invite me and my fellow Canadians out to dinner. During the meal, he offered this advice: "While in Japan, don't try to be an imitation of a Japanese. Be the best Canadian you can be."

Years later I understood what he meant. I was a coach for Canada at the Francophone Games in Madagascar. I sat and watched a team from one of the African countries just spending time together enjoying the evening by singing and dancing. I still remember, vividly, how their coordination and ease of movement, on and off the mat, impressed me. At one time it was considered an easy draw to fight someone from one of the small African nations because their judoka lacked experience. But now, by utilizing their natural great athleticism in combination with modern training methods, they are quickly becoming a force to be reckoned with at all levels of international judo. Thus it was years later that I fully understood what Mr. Okono intended.

Style dictates efficiency and thus endurance. The Japanese style is rhythmical and fluid even under the pressure of fatigue; the Russian style is powerful, controlling, calculated; the French and German are more like Russians yet the British are more traditional in the Japanese style because of the influence of the Japanese founding instructors of the Budowai in London, just as in North America, where Japanese immigrants had the greatest influence. So I now understand that where formerly judo was more culturally based, today each national judo association "cherry picks" the best techniques and creates its own style for the future.

It is in this way that the legacy of Jigoro Kano continues, through an evolving definition of sports judo. Although the transition from a traditional martial art form into match competition began in the 1870s, modern judo began with the first World Judo Championship in 1952. The process of ratification and acceptance continued with the inclusion of judo in the 1964 Olympic Games, particularly with the entry of the Eastern Bloc teams. The breakup of the Eastern European Communist Bloc after 1989 accelerated the development of the sport as greater numbers of Eastern Bloc competitors, whose fighting styles and training methods became standard, changed styles and methods of sport specific conditioning.

In competitive judo, dynamic throws are the most sought-after of all moves. Moreover, in tachi waza, judoka must pass through all gateways to accomplish the final outcome of a spectacular throw. This chapter covers the most successful throws in modern competition judo as well as the fine points of executing them and the most common errors judoka make when attempting them. The list of throws is short because I want to encourage you to learn to analyze and rate your existing judo throws and then decide whether to add a throw to or delete a throw from your repertoire. This may seem to be a complicated process, given that you have to consider a number of factors when choosing throws in which to invest your limited training time, but I have found it to be very useful.

Each throw in this chapter is analyzed according to the probability of scoring, the ease of entry, the risk of being countered, the risk of being penalized for a false attack, and the psychological advantage of having strong counters.

WALK HOW YOU WANT

Walk how you want—this is my view when teaching throwing techniques. Some judoka have become too preoccupied with the slavish imitation of judo techniques, spending far too much time on some small point of the way they walk in judo or some detail of gripping perfectly or doing static uchikomi so as to place the body in some perfected position from which to throw. Europeans have been criticized for their untraditional postures and ways of walking. But during the action of competitive judo, rarely do the principles of perfection apply. Of course the basic principles of throws must be respected, but they are very general principles, such as the requirement that the hand, shoulders, hips, and feet all drive in one direction around a general point of contact to establish a fulcrum.

Once you have acquired the basic movements for various throws, you should spend more time learning how to become a better athlete and finding your own way of walking and entering into throws by customizing your strength and your judo style to maximize the potential of your body type and physical attributes. This ideal is well demonstrated by the great success that European judoka have in international competition. The more naturally you move, while respecting basic principles, the greater your chance of success.

In fact it seems totally wrong for Caucasians, who generally have strong shoulders and arms but relatively stiff hips and knees, to imitate exactly the Japanese way of throwing. The Japanese, by contrast, tend to have stronger and more flexible hips and knees than Caucasians have, but their upper bodies tend not to be as strong.

As I teach the children at my dojo, we must do the small things the very best way we can so that doing our best becomes a habit. Such attention to detail develops concentration, stamina, and body coordination. However, for an elite fighter whose sole purpose is to win, those small details of movement and body positioning may not be necessary. Sometimes they may not even be the most efficient way to hurl someone over your back without the opponent having a chance to get a throw on you. It is a little like the exquisite Japanese tea ceremony, which is beautiful to watch and allows the practitioner to acquire many redeeming qualities. However, the most efficient way to get a cup of tea may be to grab it and drink.

If the goal of your judo is simply to win the match, then you may be able to compensate for failure in the small details by your athletic prowess. But if you are using judo as an educational tool, for preparation in your everyday life, then concentration on the smallest details, as in the tea ceremony, plays a much more important role.

We must not mix these two goals and processes when we are talking about winning for winning's sake.

THROWS

This book is intended for elite athletes; therefore, the basics of each throw are treated as understood. In most cases, the original Kano definition is used because the thrust of the book is the application of gripping and stepping techniques to obtain entry to a throw. In one sense, the throw emerges as inevitable from the sequence of obtaining a grip and gaining entry.

The rating system used in this chapter is my personal approach to the selection of throws that you may concentrate on for competition. The first criterion is the chance of scoring ippon. Statistics supplied by the IJF reveal which particular throws score ippon most often. It only makes sense to build these high-scoring throws into your repertoire.

The second criterion is the risk of being penalized for false attack. In modern judo, with athletes growing in quality, all scores are vital to the outcome of the match. The risk of being penalized for false attack is a major consideration when selecting throws to add to your repertoire. Remember, you can execute five sound drop seoi nage attacks, but if you perform the sixth one improperly, you will be penalized.

The final criterion is balancing the possibility of a high score against the risk of being countered. Depending on the entry or application of the throw, the risk of counter can be changed from high to low simply by altering the entry and application. With the IJF rules requiring judges to look for repeated positive attacks, the question of ease of entry becomes much more important.

Sotomakikomi (Outside Wrapping Throw)

Sotomakikomi is traditionally used by heavyweights, but it can be equally effective for lightweights. The throw's biggest weakness is that if you fail attempting it, you usually place uke into a good position to attack you on the ground.

Chance of scoring ippon: High

Ease of entry: High

Risk of penalty: Low

Risk of counter: Low

To apply a right-handed sotomakikomi (figure 3.1), entice uke to step forward with his right foot as you pull his right arm with your left hand and trap it under your right armpit. Once uke's balance is broken, step out with your right foot to a point between you and uke. Swing your left foot back and pivot on your right foot while ensuring good control over uke's right arm by maintaining tight contact with your side of your body by clapping tight with your upper arm. Roll uke across your lower back and down to the mat.

a *b*

c *d*

Figure 3.1 Sotomakikomi (outside wrapping throw): *(a)* uke steps forward with right foot as tori traps uke's right arm; *(b)* tori steps with right foot between himself and his opponent; *(c)* tori swings left foot back and pivots on right foot; *(d)* uke rolls across tori's back and to the mat.

> **Fine point:** You must have firm control over uke's sleeve before you attempt the throw or uke will simply retract his arm and block with his hips. This often will leave you facedown on the mat and vulnerable.

Moroto Seoi Nage

Moroto seoi nage has always been a popular throw in competition, especially with light, fast fighters. The most popular version is applied by tori dropping to one or both knees. The technique of dropping to both knees gained popularity in the mid-1970s after the Russians had such great success with it during the world championships in 1975 and the 1976 Olympics.

Chance of scoring ippon: High

Ease of entry: Moderate

Risk of penalty: Low to moderate

Risk of counter: Low

Moroto seoi nage (figure 3.2) is most commonly applied with a sleeve lapel grip. For a right-handed throw, entice uke to move toward your left front corner.

a   *b*

Figure 3.2   Moroto seoi nage: *(a)* tori pulls uke's sleeve as uke steps forward toward left front corner; *(b)* tori pulls with right hand and steps across uke's body with right foot while pulling uke onto his toes; *(c)* tori makes a large semicircle with left foot and lowers to one or both knees; *(d)* tori completes the throw.

As uke steps forward, pull on uke's sleeve. Be sure to rotate your wrist and turn your little finger up at the same time. Rotate your right hand so the back of your right hand is turned toward uke's chest.

As you pull with your left hand, step your right foot across uke's body and in front of uke's right foot. Simultaneously pull uke onto the toes of his right foot. Once you feel uke lose balance, make a large semicircle with your left foot. As you swing your hips in front of uke, lower your center of balance by dropping to either one knee or both knees.

Once you feel uke's chest make contact with your back, drive your hips up as you pull uke's sleeve across your body toward your left hip to complete the throw.

The greater control you get over both of uki's shoulders means that you would likely take uki down with you in a failed seoi nage attack, eliminating the risk of false attack penalties.

Although there are a number of different entries for seoi nage, be sure to time the entry and the control of uke's upper body by way of the pulling action so that your thumb is tucked squarely in front of your own shoulder.

Do not try to push your elbow up and under uke's armpit. If your timing is off, this action may apply undue pressure on your elbow, which may cause an injury.

c

d

Ippon Seoi Nage

Ippon seoi nage is a very strong version of seoi nage that many moroto seoi nage experts change to later in their careers, more often than not as a result of elbow injuries caused by the elbow being mispositioned during a poorly timed moroto seoi nage attempt.

> Chance of scoring ippon: High
>
> Ease of entry: Low
>
> Risk of penalty: Medium to high
>
> Risk of counter: Low

With ippon seoi nage, the entry and timing are similar to those of moroto seoi nage. Instead of keeping hold of uke's lapel, however, tori lets go of uke's lapel and hooks his right arm under uke's armpit by pinching uke's left arm between tori's forearm and bicep (figure 3.3), giving tori a great deal of control over uke's left shoulder.

A common mistake is for tori not to control uke's left shoulder sufficiently. Usually this is caused by either not pulling uke's sleeve or by not trapping uke's left arm sufficiently with the hooking action of tori's right hand.

One solution to the problem of insufficient control of uke's left shoulder is to use an unusual grip. While applying ippon seoi nage, get a grip on uke's right lapel grip over uke's arm. As you apply seoi nage, maintain your grip on uke's lapel with your left hand and grab the bottom of uke's right sleeve with your right hand. This gives you a great deal of control over uke's right shoulder. Then apply the rest of the throw as a normal drop seoi nage.

Caution: Because there is less control over both of uke's shoulders, ippon seoi nage does have a higher risk of receiving a false attack penalty if it is not performed correctly.

Figure 3.3   Ippon seoi nage.

Te Waza (Leg Grabs)

Leg grabs are becoming very popular among fighters of all sizes and both sexes. When you consider the ratings, you will see why so many fighters are adding them to their repertoires.

Chance of scoring ippon: High

Ease of entry: High

Risk of penalty: Moderate

Risk of counter: Low

There are two main types of leg grabs: a right-handed leg grab against a left-handed opponent (kenkyoko position) and a leg grab with a right-versus-right grip.

For the right-handed leg grab against a left-handed opponent (kenkyoko, figure 3.4), tori grasps the left leg of uke while seizing uke's left lapel. Tori pulls uke's lapel with his right hand while taking a step back with his right foot. Simultaneously, tori moves all of uke's weight onto the leg tori is intending to attack (in this case, the left leg). Tori cups his left hand and scoops uke's leg behind the knee to make uke's knee buckle. Tori finishes off the throw by taking a small adjustment step with his left foot between uke's legs; this movement limits tori's risk of being countered. Tori steps again with the right foot to hook the buckled leg while burying his forehead into uke's chest, landing chest-to-chest on uke.

> **Fine point:** The subtlety of this throw involves the use of the action–reaction principle. When tori pulls uke's lapel at the beginning of the throw, he carefully waits for uke to pull back in reaction before he attacks with the throw.

The most common error with te waza is that tori pushes with the hand that holds uke's lapel instead of pulling. If tori's left foot is placed well between uke's feet during the adjustment step, he prevents uke from making a counter. This same error is common with the second type of leg grab as well, the leg grab with a right-versus-right grip.

For the leg grab with right-versus-right grip (figure 3.5), if tori seizes uke's right sleeve or lapel, tori attacks uke's left leg. For a right-handed throw, tori takes a right-handed grip and steps back with his left foot, putting uke's weight on the outside blade of uke's right foot. Tori steps in with his left foot well between uke's feet. He scoops up uke's right foot and drives uke to the back corner, landing on uke chest-to-chest.

a b

Figure 3.4 Te waza, right-handed leg grab versus a left-handed opponent: *(a)* tori grasps uke's left leg; *(b)* while pulling on uke's lapel, tori steps back; *(c)* tori makes uke's knee buckle by scooping his leg; *(d)* tori completes the throw.

a b

Figure 3.5 Te waza, right-against-right grip: *(a)* tori grips with right hand and steps back with left foot; *(b)* tori steps between uke's feet; *(c)* tori scoops uke's right foot; *(d)* tori completes the throw.

c

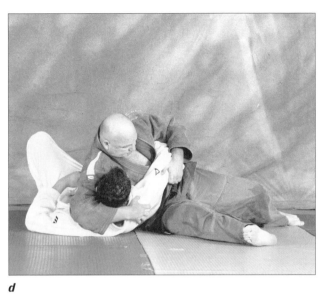

d

c

d

Fine points

1. Aggressive fighters who like a fast-paced fight often perform these two throws.

2. To avoid being countered, put your right foot between your opponent's feet. This helps bring the opponent into your body as close as possible and helps you lift your opponent's leg to avoid a counterattack. Remember, it is easier to move your own body than your opponent's.

Although the risk of penalty with te waza is moderate, it is lessened if you cup uki's knee instead of grabbing the pant leg of the gi.

Kata Guruma (Shoulder Wheel)

The relatively new popularity of the drop version of kata guruma is a significant example of how rules change fighting styles. At one time, the drop shoulder throw was by far the most common dropping attack in competitive judo. Then rule changes penalized judoka with a shido for false attack if the attacker's hips did not fully rotate or tori failed to unbalance the opponent.

In kata guruma (figure 3.6), the attack is applied from the side instead of between the legs as with the drop shoulder throw. Thus the attacker is not obliged to fully rotate his hips and there is no fear of receiving a penalty.

a   *b*

Figure 3.6   Traditional kata guruma: *(a)* tori lifts uke onto her shoulders; *(b)* tori completes the throw.

Chance of scoring ippon: Moderate to high

Ease of entry: High

Risk of penalty: Low

Risk of counter: Low

In traditional kata guruma, while breaking your opponent's balance to his right front corner, you lift him onto your shoulders and drop him on the mat. Step in as deeply as possible with your right foot. The back of your head should be at the right side of your opponent's belt.

For a drop kata guruma using a right-to-right grip (figure 3.7), from a right-handed sleeve lapel grip tori entices uke to step forward with the right foot as tori pulls on uke's right sleeve. The moment tori feels uke's weight shift onto the right foot, tori slips his left foot out to a hurdler's stretch position while slipping his head into uke's armpit and pulling down on the sleeve to ensure tight body contact. Tori's right hand wraps around uke's upper thigh to control the finish of the throw.

a

b

Figure 3.7 Drop kata guruma, right-to-right grip: *(a)* tori pulls uke's right sleeve as uke steps forward; *(b)* tori takes a hurdler stretch position and puts her head into uke's armpit; *(c)* tori completes the throw.

c

The left-to-right grip for a drop kata guruma is often awkward. During the grip-ping process, both sides work hard to catch the opponent's sleeve. This provides a great opportunity to apply a double-kneed drop kata guruma (figure 3.8). Tori grabs uke's left sleeve near the triceps. Tori then pulls with his right hand (which is holding uke's upper sleeve) while rotating and dropping his body between uke's feet. After landing on both knees simultaneously, tori tucks his head under uke's armpit while wrapping his left arm around uke's upper thigh.

a   *b*   *c*

Figure 3.8   Double-kneed drop kata guruma: *(a)* tori grasps uke's sleeve and pulls; *(b)* tori drops between uke's feet, landing on both knees, and puts her head into uke's armpit, wrapping her arm around uke's thigh; *(c)* tori completes the throw.

> **Fine point:** Timing is critical to the completion of this throw, but the ability to disappear under your opponent's center of balance will come with relatively little practice compared to the skills needed for more complicated throws such as uchimata or foot sweeps. Because of the ease of entry and the low risk of being penalized for false attack, this throw should play a major role in tactical aspects of a match.

The most common error with this throw is that tori fails to keep control of uke's shoulder. Tori must apply a strong downward pull to ensure that uke's weight is on the side that tori attacks.

Ouchigari (Major Inner Reaping)

Ouchigari is a very valuable tool if used correctly. Not only does it have a reasonably high success rate in achieving some kind of score, but also the ease of entry and the many opportunities available to use it enable the development of a solid tactical plan.

A word of caution: Because ouchigari is easy to apply, a halfhearted or poorly executed attack could easily result in your looking up at your opponent on the wrong end of a counter.

Chance of scoring ippon: Low to moderate

Ease of entry: High

Risk of penalty: Low

Risk of counter: Low to high

The risk of counter with ouchigari depends on what style you employ. The risk can be lessened by ensuring that your belt is well below your opponent's and by paying attention to which of your opponent's shoulders you look over as you attack. If you look over the shoulder on the side you are hooking, your chance of getting a higher score increases but so does your chance of being countered.

For the original Kano ouchigari technique (figure 3.9), after breaking your opponent's balance to his left back corner, reap his left leg from the inside with your right leg so that he falls backward. Be sure to twist your hips to the left as you attack so that you can insert your right leg heel first, toes pointed in, and reap widely to the right.

Unless you decide to become an ouchigari expert, try the following version, which requires you to look over the left shoulder as you attack on the right, or vice versa.

Figure 3.9 Original ouchigari technique.

From a sleeve and lapel grip applied in this case with a right-handed attack on a right-handed opponent, tori pulls uke in a circular motion so that uke's weight is on the right foot (figure 3.10). Simultaneously, uke takes a small adjustment step to ensure that tori's right foot makes a triangle with uke's feet. Tori brings in the left foot to make a T with tori's two feet, in a movement similar to a fencer's stance before lunging. Simultaneously, tori lowers his right elbow and with his right hand pulls uke's left wrist to tori's right hip, thus keeping uke's weight on the right foot. It is vital that tori does not twist his body or bring his left foot past his right foot. Otherwise, tori puts himself at risk of being countered.

Tori now makes a large reaping action with his right leg, hooking uke's calf with his own calf. Before making contact, tori lowers his hips below uke's belt while looking over and driving through uke's right shoulder. To finish the throw, tori drives his opponent straight back and lands chest-to-chest on uke.

a   *b*   *c*

Figure 3.10   Modified ouchigari technique: *(a)* tori pulls uke in circular motion; *(b)* tori moves into a fencer's stance; *(c)* tori reaps with his right leg.

Fine point: As tori's and uke's calves make contact, tori's reaping foot forms a semicircle from the big toe to the heel, creating the ideal reaping instrument and keeping the weight of both judoka on the proper side.

A common mistake is for tori to push uke back with the lapel arm instead of in and down with it.

Kouchigari (Minor Inner Reaping)

Kouchigari is an extremely versatile throw that can be done in right-to-right stance or right-to-left stance. It often is thought of as a setup throw for combinations or a throw to secure a small score. In the right hands, however, it can be a deadly tool that suddenly ends a match. When used with precision timing, it can negate the advantages of a stronger opponent.

Chance of scoring ippon: Moderate to low

Ease of entry: High

Risk of penalty: Low

Risk of counter: Low

This description of the throw is Kano's. It is interesting to note that a Japanese teacher will give the generic example first, and then, if asked, may show his own version.

After breaking your opponent's balance to his right back corner, reap his right foot from the inside with your right foot and throw him backward (figure 3.11). Timing is crucial. Ideally you skim the mat with the sole of your right foot, being sure to reap with your big toe curled inward. In any case, push your opponent's foot forward, not up, with the little-toe side of your foot brushing the mat.

In competition, the stepping-away entry in an opposite stance is the most common, although for setups or to keep your opponent slightly off balance, any of the various entries are useful.

Figure 3.11 Kouchigari.

Fine point: In the stepping-away entry, the action of pulling your sleeve hand into your hip strengthens the pulling and rotation moment necessary to complete the throw.

I have witnessed the extremely talented Jason Morris from the USA throw a much stronger opponent at the world championships for wazari with a kouchigari. Jason had no grip at all but performed the throw only with the use of precise timing and by directing his opponent's shoulders with his open hands. It was one of the highlights of that competition.

A common error is to push the opponent away. This will only push him back on balance. Tori must use a drawing action as opposed to a driving action.

Osotogari (Major Outer Reaping)

Osotogari is an extremely powerful throw that adapts well in the awkward right-versus-left stance situation. As with any one-legged throw, if it is done halfheart-edly the risk of being countered looms. However, if tori breaks uke's balance before committing to the attack, the risk of being countered is outweighed by the high success rate of this throw.

Chance of scoring ippon: High

Ease of entry: High

Risk of penalty: Low

Risk of counter: Moderate

Break your opponent's balance toward his right back corner, causing him to shift all of his weight toward his right heel (figure 3.12). Reap his right leg with your right leg. Step as far left of his right foot as you can so that you can put power into the reaping action.

a   *b*

Figure 3.12 Osotogari: *(a)* tori breaks uke's balance toward uke's right back corner; *(b)* tori reaps uke's right leg with his right leg.

Fine point: To ensure a strong finish, tuck your chin inward and down. Keep the thumb of your right hand in front of your own right shoulder.

A common error is for tori to attack before uke's balance is broken, putting tori at risk of being countered. To avoid this situation, tori must ensure that uke's balance is completely broken to his right back corner by tori's body movement before his leg comes in contact with uke's leg.

Uchimata (Inner Thigh Reaping)

Uchimata is without a doubt the most versatile and effective throw in modern competitive judo. All competitors at the national and international levels should have some version of this popular throw in their repertoires.

Because of the wide variety of possible entries, this throw is difficult to rate. The risk of counter ranges from extremely high in the case of the spinning entry to very low in the case of the French double-stab uchimata. One thing is sure: The chances of scoring with uchimata have always been high.

Chance of scoring ippon: High

Ease of entry: Low to moderate

Risk of penalty: Low

Risk of counter: Low to high

After breaking your opponent's balance to his front or to his right front corner, sweep his inner thigh from within with the back of your right thigh (hamstring) (figure 3.13). Execute the throw as your opponent's weight is shifting to his left foot. In this version, you slide your left leg between your opponent's legs. Your left foot should point in the opposite direction to your opponent's right foot.

Figure 3.13 Uchimata.

Fine point: Tori's support leg must be bent and driving. The toes of the hooking foot must be pointing out because in some cases tori might actually hook uke's leg with his foot.

A common error is for tori to attack uke before uke's balance is fully broken. This is dangerous in most throws, but with the full-body commitment needed to complete this one-legged throw, complete kuzushi is imperative. Much concentration on setups and the entry to this throw is needed. Remember, by using his hands and body to break uke's balance before hooking uke's leg, tori dramatically improves his chances of a successful throw.

The Sound of Uchikomi

As a judo competitor, you will come in contact with many amazing people who will have unique and fascinating ways of looking at our sport. If you can keep an open mind to new ideas and interpretations, you will acquire a deeper understanding of judo.

One such amazing person is Dr. Ken Kingsbury. For approximately 30 years, Ken was the British judo team doctor. His contribution to the team constituted of much more than just medical advice. Ken had a great deal of input into the design of the team's conditioning and training methods in the 1970s and 1980s, a period considered by many to be British judo's heyday.

At the 1972 Olympics, Ken was watching the Japanese team warm up. During their uchikomi, he noticed a distinctive sound difference between the emphasis, or rhythm, of the movement of the feet of the Japanese team and that of the British team during uchikomi. Ken audiotaped the two teams while they did uchikomi. The Japanese foot pattern was "soft, heavy, heavy" (pat, thud, thud). The first, "soft" step was tori's foot stepping to the head of the triangle; the next, louder, more forceful step was the rotation step; and the final step was another powerful step to complete the throw. This pattern ensured that once tori was in place for the throw, he had a lot of power left in the movement to finish the throw.

Many of the British team competitors had a "heavy, heavy, soft" foot pattern (thud, thud, pat). The first step to the head of the triangle was strong and powerful, the second step was an equally strong rotation step, and the third step was softer. They had little power left in the action to finish the throw.

This analysis of step rhythm may seem insignificant, but the rhythm of the British foot pattern, which is common throughout Europe and North America, has strong implications for the result of the throw. With our strong upper bodies, we try to pull the opponent right off his feet from the first step and then follow with an equally strong rotation step, leaving little control left to apply the final stage of the throw or to maintain balance to apply a second drive if necessary. The consequence of using the Western foot pattern is that if tori is unsuccessful at pulling uke to a point of no return on the first step, the throw often fails. With the poor control left in the last step, tori often ends up on his face in groundwork.

Of course not all British, European, or North American judoka use this step pattern, but it is fair to say that enough do to validate the scenario described. Think about this when you practice uchikomi.

THROW COUNTERS

It takes a special type of fighter to be really effective at countering uke's attempted throw. To understand counters, one must have a deep understanding of body positioning, grip control, and off-balancing, as well as the particular throw uke uses and the appropriate counter throw. But that just covers the physical aspect to counters.

There is a big difference between a judoka who takes advantage of uke's griev-ous mistake during an attack to knock uke down for a score and a judoka who can sense uke preparing for an attack, can control the grips and momentum of uke's attack, and can use those movements as the basis for a counterattack.

As well as understanding the physical aspects of judo, the counter specialist must have the confidence and clarity to recognize, based on uke's grip and movements, what throws uke is likely to attempt and then react effectively. Only sustained rehearsal in drills for specific situations followed by appropri-ate randori will develop such insights.

The simple fact is that a judoka's reputation, particularly for counters, has a profound effect on many of his opponents. Opponents who fear being countered often do not attack as frequently, or with as much commitment, as they might otherwise.

Drills for Counters

Drills are the first step to making counters efficient and automatic. Drilling will not only perfect the technical aspect of the counter, but it will also develop the timing and coordination of the muscles to enable you to apply the counter effectively. The following drills will help you develop a feel for counters. Each drill achieves a different objective in the process of learning throw counters.

Drill 1: The Power of Letting Go

The objective of drill 1 is to help you understand the power of letting go of uke's lapel. First take a sleeve lapel grip. Ask uke to turn in for a major forward throw such as taiotoshi, haraigoshi, or seoi nage. For the first few attacks, keep holding on to uke's lapel. Feel how the rotation of your partner's body pulls you off balance.

Now ask uke to let go of your sleeve but still rotate his body just as much as he did before. It may surprise you to discover that as long as you maintain a hold on uke's lapel as he rotates to attack, you are helping to pull yourself off balance!

Now ask your partner to attack as they maintain a sleeve grip. Simply let go of uke's lapel and bring your elbow into your own hip. The simple act of letting go of your opponent's lapel and tucking your elbow to your hip keeps your shoulders square and allows you to maintain your balance.

This drill seems simple, but it clearly demonstrates how you might assist in knocking yourself off balance by holding on to the opponent's gi at all costs. This drill should be part of every judoka's uchikomi routine until it is instinctive.

Drill 2: The Pushing-Away Technique

The objective of drill 2 is to rehearse a variety of counters in uchikomi. Try to get a feel for how to negate your opponent's kuzushi (attempt to unbal-ance you). During moving uchikomi, ask your partner to attack in a forward major throw. As your partner turns in for the throw, let go of his lapel, tuck your elbow in toward your body, and bring your hand around his shoulder, cupping your hand flat on his shoulder blade. Attack with kosotogari against his far leg.

> **Fine point:** Keeping your hips low and behind uke, step your right leg between your partner's legs as you shift your weight into the throw.

Drill 3: The Cowboy Drill

The objective of the final drill is to rehearse evasion and throw blocking. It takes a lot of confidence to be proficient at counters, and you need to develop an ability to ride out throws. This drill helps you use only your body to avoid being thrown. When you become more efficient, you may even be able to block your opponent's throws in this manner.

Ask your opponent to attack repeatedly in randori fashion with a specific throw. Do not hold on to your opponent's gi. Use only your body and movement to stop or evade the throw. Start with your opponent holding a sleeve lapel grip. As you become more proficient at this drill, progress to a double lapel grip and then to a sleeve collar grip. When you get good at defending specified throws, try open randori (attacking with any throw) in the same manner.

> **Fine point:** Keep a slight bend in your knees. Aim at using the smallest possible body movements to thwart your opponent's attempt to unbalance you.

Avoidance Counters

Specific avoidance counters demonstrate the most basic principle of judo—use your opponent's power against himself. With little or no effort, you hurl an opponent to the ground simply by getting out of the way and redirecting his force.

Subame Gaeshi

Subame gaeshi (figure 3.14) is also called the swallow throw after the swooping movement of the bird.

Your opponent attacks you with a foot sweep. Simply remove your foot in a circular manner and sweep your opponent's foot as you pull down on his gi with the hand that corresponds to the side of the sweeping foot.

> **Fine point:** While executing the counter, sweep either uke's sweeping foot or his support foot. Often it is easier and more effective to go after uke's support foot.

a   *b*

Figure 3.14 Tsubame gaeshi: *(a)* uke attacks with a foot sweep; *(b)* tori circles his foot and sweeps uke's foot while pulling down on uke's gi.

A common mistake is to lift the sweeping leg from the hip. The movement must come from the knee down. To do tsubame gaeshi, you must have no bending of the hips.

While at Budo University in Japan, I had considerable success with this counter until I met Kashiwazaki Sensei, under whom I had studied for a year in England. On this occasion, the randori started and Kashiwazaki attempted an uncharacteristically slow foot sweep on me. I knew this was my chance to get a rare score on the one-time world champion. I blasted in with my tsubame gaeshi counter only to find myself crashing to the mat as my tsubame gaeshi was countered by Kashiwazaki's tsubame gaeshi counter to my own counter. We both laughed as he told me he had been planning it for days while watching me catch his students with my counter. He had been scouting my techniques!

Uchimata Sukashi

As your opponent attempts uchimata, sidestep his sweeping leg while using your hand action to sustain his circular momentum (figure 3.15). At the same time, step across your opponent's body in a taiotoshi movement.

Fine point: The success of the sukashi counter depends on your hand movement continuing uke's self-propelled momentum.

a   b

Figure 3.15 Uchimata sukashi: *(a)* tori steps away from uke's attempt at uchimata; *(b)* tori steps across uke in taiotoshi.

Counter to Leg Grabs

Awareness is the first key to avoid being thrown by leg grabs. You must become familiar with the various forms of leg grabs to stop the attacker as he goes to grab your leg. To get to your leg, your opponent must bend down. As he does, use his poor posture to drag him forward until he falls onto his knees. The better your own posture is, the easier the task will be.

Osotogari Countered by Osotogari

In competition, one of the most common and exploitable situations in which to use osotogari in attack occurs when one fighter is dominating with a sleeve high collar grip and the controlled judoka is bent at the waist. If you are the controlled judoka and your opponent has a high collar grip, step into your opponent's push with your hip to maintain an upright posture (figure 3.16a). Then drop your sleeve hand from uke's elbow to the body of his gi just above his belt, which will enable you to pull his hip toward you (figure 3.16b). If uke tries osotogari, take a small step outward with your free foot and rotate your hips as you would in a taiotoshi position while pulling in toward your body with both hands. When you feel uke go off balance, continue the rotation by reaping your leg in osotogari fashion (figure 3.16c). Try to end with a makikomi finish (figure 3.16d).

a

b

c

d

Figure 3.16 Osotogari countered by osotogari: *(a)* tori steps into uke to maintain an upright posture; *(b)* tori pulls uke's hip toward him; *(c)* tori reaps his legs in osotogari; *(d)* tori finishes in makikomi.

Fine point: Keeping your toes pointing out (away from uke) increases your chance of success.

While in a high-collar-to-high-collar gripping situation, do not let your thumb drift behind your shoulder.

4

Holds, Chokes, and Armlocks

At one time newaza was not fashionable, and even today some elite judoka lack experience and skill in groundwork. But in fact, newaza is a very powerful set of techniques, and many matches are won on the ground.

I find it interesting that it was not even the sport of judo that brought widespread awareness to many of the ground moves covered in this chapter. It was a ju jitsu practitioner, Renzio Gracie, with his success in mixed martial arts who, using his considerable grappling skills, obtained submission after submission from opponents, many of whom were much larger and stronger than he was.

For a competitive judoka's training, newaza offers a number of benefits. In addition to the obvious benefit of adding powerful scoring tools to your judo repertoire, newaza is also a remarkably effective strengthening and conditioning tool. Perhaps the greatest value, however, is the psychological edge it provides: When your opponent is aware of your expertise on the ground, he is often a little more hesitant in attacking you with a deeply committed throw, lest you turn his failed attack to your advantage on the ground. With this in mind, I suggest that judoka after the grade of green belt should be familiar with the basic grappling techniques covered in this chapter. They are the most common and effective grappling moves in competitive judo.

A judoka must consider several factors when developing groundwork techniques. Just as the chapter on throwing techniques listed the criteria for the choice or ranking of throws, this chapter lists the criteria that make ground techniques effective in competition, including

- the ease of entry from given throws or takedowns,
- the effectiveness of the technique, and
- the ease with which judoka can move from one technique to another.

The traditional way to study groundwork is first to become proficient at hold-downs, then at chokes, and finally at armlocks. This is a sound progression from a safety standpoint, giving tori time to develop control over uke's movement. Also, by learning hold-downs first, tori learns to control uke's body before he tries the potentially more dangerous chokes or armlocks. Control over uke's body is vital to the successful completion of these techniques. Unfortunately, today judoka starting judo at a later age don't learn the hold-downs as thoroughly. Because armlocks and chokes are allowed at a younger age, many do not concentrate as much on becoming proficient at hold-downs before progressing to chokes and armlocks. Training to be proficient at hold-downs does take time. But the skills obtained in newaza will serve you well with all of your judo techniques.

HOLDS

In the section on holds, I cover four of the most common holds used in competition today. If you can master these four basic holds, you can create a solid base from which to build your complete newaza repertoire.

Earlier I discussed learning holds first from the safety aspect of the sport, but there is a great tactical reason to look to apply one of these holds. If you secure a hold, you are more than likely going to hold on for the 25 seconds to gain ippon. Even if you do not secure ippon, even if you do not secure the hold, uke is very likely to get into a vulnerable position for a choke or armlock in an attempt to avoid the pin.

Kesa Gatame (Scarf Hold)

Approaching your opponent from his left side, sit with your hip firmly against his side so that there is no space between you. Wrap your right arm over uke's left arm and grip his judogi at the armpit. It is important to make sure that uke's left arm is tightly secured under your own armpit. Place your left arm around his neck like a scarf and grip the left shoulder of his judogi (figure 4.1). Thrust your left leg forward and your top (right) leg back.

Fine point: It is very important that there be no space or gap between uke's body and your hip and side. Adjust your position as your opponent moves.

Figure 4.1 Kesa gatame (scarf hold).

A common mistake is not controlling uke's forearm in your own armpit by squeezing your upper arm against your body.

Kata Gatame (Shoulder Hold)

In an attempt to escape from your kesa gatame, uke may try to free his trapped arm from beneath your armpit. If so, as your opponent frees his arm from your armpit, take the arm with your own left hand and push his liberated arm across his face (figure 4.2). Drop your head down, placing your own right ear tightly against uke's right ear, and then clasp your hands together. Your legs may remain in the same position or come up on your right shin. Place your right knee tightly into uke's side, blocking him from turning in. Put your weight on your left foot, thus forcing your weight onto your opponent.

A common mistake is to allow space between your ear and uke's ear, thus permitting uke to wedge his elbow into the space and increase the gap, possibly enabling him to escape.

Figure 4.2 Kata gatame (shoulder hold).

Tateshiho Gatame

Sitting astride uke's body, tori lies forward across uke's chest (figure 4.3a). Tori then places his right arm under uke's head and secures uke's head by taking uke's right lapel and feeding the lapel under uke's right armpit (figure 4.3b). Tori then transfers the lapel to his right hand and tightens up any slack.

a   b

Figure 4.3   Tateshiho gatame: *(a)* tori lies across uke's chest; *(b)* tori secures uke's head and tightens any slack.

Fine point: Tori's head and left hand should be free to establish a tripod position for balance and stability as uke tries to escape. Thus, you can use your shoulder to pin uke's head in the direction of your free hand so that you can use that hand to block uke's bridging action.

Yokoshiho Gatame (Side Forecorner Hold): Orthodox Position

As your opponent is lying on his back, approach him from the side. Place your left arm around and under his neck and grip his left shoulder. Place your right hand between his legs and grasp the skirt of the jacket (figure 4.4). To stop him from turning in and sliding his right leg between your legs, place your right knee against his waist and press down on him with your body. As your opponent moves to escape, you will have to adjust the position of your hips and legs. You should control his bridging action by pressuring his head with your left shoulder.

Fine point: Be sure to hold uke's jacket skirt low enough so that uke does not have a good angle to use the power of his legs to break your grip on the skirt of the judogi.

Figure 4.4 Yokoshiho gatame (side forecorner hold): orthodox position.

Be careful that you do not allow your opponent to force your head down toward his legs or he will be free to push the back of your head down toward his belt. He could then attempt to hook your head and arm with his legs and attempt a sangaku-jime attack.

Yokoshiho Gatame: Wilhelm Ruska's Version

In Ruska's version of yokoshiho gatame (figure 4.5), instead of gripping between uke's legs, tori slips his right hand under the small of uke's back and grabs the end of the skirt of uke's judogi. With his left hand over uke's left shoulder, tori grabs uke's belt. In this hybrid combination of yokoshiho gatame and kamishiho gatame, tori lays his chest in a diagonal fashion over uke's left shoulder.

Figure 4.5 Yokoshiho gatame: Wilhelm Ruska's version.

Fine point: Tori controls uke's escaping action by controlling uke's hips with his left arm, and uke's attempts to bridge by applying force with his body on uke's left shoulder.

Kamishiho Gatame (Upper Forecorner Hold)

When your opponent is lying on his back, approach him from his head. Lay chest to chest. Your arm should slide under his shoulders and reach down to grab hold of his belt (figure 4.6). Pull yourself into uke while pulling uke up to you. Your abdomen should be positioned on his face, smothering him and forcing him to turn his head to one side. Push your hip down on his head. You have now eliminated one direction of escape. Your legs may be in either of two positions: stretched out and spread behind you or bent underneath you. Adjust as your opponent moves.

Figure 4.6 Kamishiho gatame (upper forecorner hold).

> **Fine point:** Tori often has more control when he has one hand under uke's shoulder and the other over uke's other shoulder with each hand grabbing onto uke's belt.

Do not allow uke to gain increasing amounts of space. Adapt to uke's bridging and twisting movements.

CHOKES

Choking is a great equalizer. A small man with thin wrists can subdue a much larger and more powerful man by using little or no strength. By employing the qualities of control over uke's body that you obtain when learning holddowns, it is easy to transfer the controlling qualities of a pin to controlling uke's body faceup or facedown and then applying a choke.

Before applying a choke, make sure you control the body. *Choke the body before you choke the neck.* As a young fighter, I often fought the open weight category at a body weight of about 154 pounds (70 kilograms), frequently competing with men who weighed in at over 220 pounds (100 kilograms). The safest strategy when facing such a mismatch of sizes was to take an opponent down onto his face, mount his back, and then apply a choke, in my case often hadake-jime. With this technique not only can uke not see what you are doing, but it's also virtually impossible for him to score against you without his reversing the situation.

Hadake-Jime (Naked Strangle)

Hadake-jime is also called the naked strangle because uke's gi is not used to apply the choke. You simply use your bare wrist. As I have suggested, this choke is usually applied when uke is facedown. Control uke's body by straddling uke (figure 4.7a). Push down on the back of uke's collar with one hand. Reach back while you are still facing forward and lift uke's leg. Slip one of your legs under uke's leg and then switch arms and do the same on the other side. Once both legs are hooked, grab both of uke's elbows. As you rock your hips forward, pull uke's elbows back toward your hips (figure 4.7b). As you feel uke's back arch, let go of one of uke's elbows and immediately slip your free hand under uke's chin (figure 4.7c). If you are successful, then immediately follow up with your other hand. Keep control over uke's body by holding uke's legs up with your own. Apply the strangle by pulling back with your wrist while applying a scooping action on the front of uke's throat.

a   b

c

Figure 4.7   Hadake-jime: *(a)* tori controls uke's body by straddling him; *(b)* tori hooks both of uke's legs and grabs uke's elbows; *(c)* once uke's back arches, tori releases one elbow and grabs uke's chin.

Fine point: As you stretch uke's legs out and arch the small of his back, his head will momentarily pop up. Try to time this initial movement so that as uke's head rocks up, you drive your hand under uke's chin.

When tori has uke stretched out, tori must be careful not to release pressure from uke's back by allowing uke's knees to touch the mat.

As you go under uke's chin with your wrist, often uke will grab your wrist. The common mistake is to try to withdraw your wrist from under uke's chin. Instead, simply grab uke's hand, leaving your wrist in place, and quickly slide your opposite hand down uke's jawline and under his chin. Grab your own wrist and then apply a scooping action to complete the choke.

Koshi-Jime (Hip Choke)

Koshi-jime (hip choke) is applied when uke is facedown. Kneel down beside uke and grab uke's belt and the back of his collar (figure 4.8a). Thrust uke forward to stretch him out while keeping pressure on his neck and back. Slip your right hand under his neck and grip his opposite lapel (figure 4.8b). Take your left hand off his belt and place it over the side of his back so as to slip under his left armpit and cup his left wrist (figure 4.8c). With your knees keeping pressure on your opponent, push off with your right leg and slip your left leg through to a sitting position so that your left hip is placed in front of his right shoulder in the gap by his neck (figure 4.8d). Apply the strangle by turning your wrist sideways, thus pushing the thumb side of your hand against his carotid artery. Pull his lapel toward you. With your left hand, pull his forearm into his left side, preventing uke from moving away. Now walk your legs around in front of his head, keeping tight to the space between his shoulder and neck.

Fine points

1. Your opponent will try to get to his knees and stand up. You must avoid this situation. The choke is much more effective if you keep uke flattened on his chest.

2. Koshi-jime can be applied as a transitional movement from standing to newaza when you have blocked your opponent's drop seoi nage.

Do not walk so fast that you raise your hips, allowing uke to roll you over his body and into a pin by trapping your arm.

a

b

c

d

Figure 4.8 Koshi-jime (hip choke): *(a)* tori kneels beside uke and grabs her belt and the back of her collar; *(b)* after stretching uke out, tori reaches under uke's neck to grip the opposite lapel; *(c)* tori reaches under uke's left arm and cups her left wrist; *(d)* tori shifts her legs to a sitting position so her left hip is in front of uke's right shoulder.

Okuri-Eri-Jime (Sliding Lapel Strangle)

From behind your opponent, stretch out uke as described in hadake-jime. Grip your opponent's left lapel under the armpit with your right hand and pull uke's lapel down toward his belt with your right hand (figure 4.9a). Bring your left hand across uke's throat and grab the taut lapel with your left hand (figure 4.9b); then let go of uke's lapel with your right hand and grab uke's right lapel. Apply the choke by pulling uke's right lapel down toward his belt (figure 4.9c).

This strangle may be applied when you are on your back or your opponent is on his belly. Always control your opponent's trunk with your body regardless of whether uke is facing up or down.

Fine point: The effectiveness of this choke is influenced more by the downward action on uke's lapel than the cross action of the lapel across the neck.

a

b

c

Figure 4.9 Okuri-eri-jime (sliding lapel strangle): *(a)* after stretching uke out, tori grabs uke's left lapel and pulls down toward his belt; *(b)* tori reaches across uke's throat and grabs the lapel with the left hand; *(c)* tori grabs uke's right lapel and pulls down toward his belt.

Sangaku-Jime (Three-Sided Strangle)

Throughout your judo career, certain moves or techniques will just click because of either your physical makeup or your fighting style. One such occasion occurred with a friend of mine, Kevin West. Kevin was very young at the time and had no national ranking or any international experience. Nevertheless, he was selected to attend the 1982 German Open as part of the Ontario Provincial team. He was introduced to the sangaku-jime just a few days before the competition, and because it felt right for him, he decided to try it during the tournament. His division—143 pounds (65 kilograms)—was very large, with almost 45 competitors, and he had seven fights. He was the unexpected winner of the gold medal in this very difficult competition, winning six out of seven matches with his newly acquired sangaku-jime technique.

Sangaku-jime is the three-sided strangle or the triangular strangle. The basic competitive sangaku-jime is executed with your opponent either lying on his belly or kneeling on his hands and knees. Begin by positioning yourself facing his head. With your right hand, grip his left sleeve below the elbow (figure 4.10a). Your left hand is on his belt at his back. Thrust your left knee into the space between your opponent's neck and shoulder on his right side, so that your knee is firmly against his ear (figure 4.10b). Step over uke's head and dig your left heel into the gap behind his right arm (figure 4.10c). It is very important that your heels are together to ensure good control and position. Roll to your left side and begin to pull your opponent's left arm (figure 4.10d). Do not allow your heels to separate. As you go onto your side, slip your right foot and ankle behind your left (bottom) knee and bend it up toward your buttocks.

To make the position more secure (there are always small gaps and spaces once you have rolled onto your side), pull on your opponent's right arm and tighten your legs again (figure 4.10e). Your left thigh (the bottom leg) then becomes like a pillow. Now secure uke's arm, using his belt or his judogi skirt and control the entire left side of his body. You can then apply pressure with your thighs for the strangle submission. Turn your hips upward toward the ceiling for extra pressure.

Fine point: Once you are in this position, you may apply an armlock or rise up over your opponent's body and apply a hold-down.

Sangaku-jime can also be successfully applied from behind your opponent when he is facedown by inserting your right arm underneath his right armpit and cupping his wrist. Stepping over his body, move around toward your right to place yourself at the beginning of the sangaku as described.

Figure 4.10 Sangaku-jime (three-sided strangle): *(a)* tori faces uke's head and grips his left sleeve below the elbow; *(b)* tori puts his knee between uke's neck and shoulder on the right; *(c)* tori steps over uke and puts his heel behind uke's right arm; *(d)* tori rolls and pulls uke's left arm; *(e)* tori secures uke's arm and applies the strangle.

LOCKS

Locks are versatile, being effective both in groundwork and as a standing technique. At one time it was legal to perform locks against the knee, but this technique was found to lead to severe injuries. Because of the risks, leg locks are not considered acceptable for use in randori or in competition, although leg locks are performed in kata today. With the rule requiring immediate progression in newaza (article 16, page 8), armlocks have become dramatically more popular in competition over the last two decades because most armlocks are applied immediately following the transition into groundwork.

Ude Garame (Arm Hold, Standing and Ground)

Ude garame is a very effective armlock for an opportunistic fighter. It can be applied when uke is beneath you or on top and between your legs. As you will see in chapter 6, it can be applied effectively during tachi waza (see page 112).

Ude garame is usually applied when uke carelessly reaches out to grab your collar with a straight arm. When uke does this, tori pinches uke's wrist in the side of tori's neck (figure 4.11a), using the combination of tori bringing his ear and shoulder together to create a V shape. At the same time, tori reaches over with his left hand and cups the elbow of uke's outstretched arm. Tori follows up with his other hand and applies pressure on uke's elbow (figure 4.11b).

Figure 4.11   Ude garame: *(a)* tori traps uke's wrist in the side of tori's neck; *(b)* tori uses the other hand to apply pressure on uke's elbow.

Fine point: Tori should rotate uke's arm so that uke's little finger is pointing away from tori's shoulder.

Don't make the common mistake of trying to apply pressure before uke's arm is fully extended.

Juji Gatame (Straight Armlock)

In basic juji gatame (or basic juji, as it is known), uke is usually on his back, faceup. This situation can arise from tori throwing uke for a partial throw or from a number of elaborate turnovers. Once tori has uke on his back, tori's legs lie across uke's chest facing up, with uke's arm outstretched between tori's legs (figure 4.12a), which are diagonally across uke's body. To apply pressure to uke's elbow, tori raises his own hips (figure 4.12b).

Figure 4.12   Juji gatame (straight armlock): *(a)* uke's arm is stretched between tori's legs as tori lies across uke's chest; *(b)* tori applies pressure to uke's elbow by lifting his hips.

Fine point: Tori must ensure that uke's elbow and little finger are in line as he applies pressure to uke's elbow.

It is common for beginners to allow their legs to separate as they apply pressure. This is a grave mistake because it allows uke to twist out of the armlock.

Judoka can choose different variations of juji gatame. Often in judo the ideal and the practical techniques meld together, so that you are sometimes unsure where they came from! The juji turnover is one such technique.

For the juji turnover, start on your back with uke between your legs. Pull uke up toward your upper body as far as possible. With your left hand, grab uke's inside sleeve by the biceps (figure 4.13a). With your right hand, reach down and grab the inseam of uke's pant leg. Again pull uke toward your head, but this time swing your hip so that you are perpendicular with uke (figure 4.13b). With your hamstring, rock uke over onto his back in a diagonal direction, assisting this movement by using your grip on uke's inseam. Instead of letting go of uke's leg as in normal juji, reach deeper through uke's leg and trap his leg in your bent elbow (figure 4.13c). Use the same hand to grab uke's wrist. Finish with your head close to uke's hips with his right arm between your legs and his left leg trapped and across his right leg.

a

b

c

Figure 4.13 Juji turnover: *(a)* tori pulls uke up and grabs uke's inside sleeve with his left hand; *(b)* tori rocks uke to his back; *(c)* tori traps uke's leg in his bent elbow and grabs uke's wrist.

Fine point: Snug your body close to uke's body and use the strength of your hamstrings to straighten uke's arms.

Often uke will trap tori's leg between his own to defend against juji. If you apply traditional juji in this instance and lean toward uke's head, often uke will escape because of the gap between your legs. If you lie on your side and grab uke's far ankle and then apply juji as described, your legs can remain tight and you can control uke.

PART II

Tactics and Strategy

5

Setting Up
a Throw Attack

Some 30 years ago, while a member of the British judo team, I first realized the importance of the grip, setup, and throw gateways and just how much they were dependent on each other for a successful outcome. At that time, I had the pleasure of training with some extremely talented judoka who regularly spent hours in practice performing uchikomi in throwing and groundwork drills. While preparing for the Moscow Olympics, the team's weekly routine included four separate 1-hour sessions of uchikomi, which included gripping drills combined with setup drills for specific throws and ground moves.

During these sessions I sometimes had the pleasure to be paired with Neil Adams, who won silver at the Moscow and Los Angeles Olympics. He also became a world champion. Neil was known at that time throughout the judo world for his throwing ability. To this day, it impresses me how seamlessly Neil could change his grips, entice his opponent to step automatically in the direction Neil wanted him to go, spin under his opponent for an attack, then come back out and start the whole process again. He displayed this skill against me often during uchikomi drills and setup drills.

Over the years I have watched Neil compete at many levels of competition, from the nationals to the Olympic Games. Throughout these competitions, I have enjoyed watching Neil successfully apply the grips, setups, and throws that he spent many tough hours perfecting.

In this chapter I describe similar setups that you can combine with your throws. Learn and practice these setups so you can use the seamless application of your grips and setups in conjunction with your favorite throws.

Practice until this skill becomes a natural and automatic part of your competitive judo repertoire.

Throughout this book I refer to gateways; a setup is one such gateway. After you attain your grip, the setup for the throw would be the next gate. A setup for a throw can be as simple as enticing uke to circle around you, as discussed later in this chapter, or as complete as fully spinning in for one throw, hoping to get a strong defensive action from uke, thus putting uke into a vulnerable state in a different direction so that you can then capitalize on his disadvantage.

Depending on uke's reaction to your setup, you then proceed to the next gateway. This gateway would be the application of the appropriate throw for uke's reaction to your setup, chosen from your repertoire of throws. In fact, I believe that this is the main quality enabling top judoka to throw in the heat of a contest. Once they step to the right place during the setup, the body takes over and they automatically apply their throws.

Under the pressure of top competition, an attack must be smooth and automatic. This is best achieved by either manipulating your opponent into a vulnerable stance or moving your body to a favorable throwing position. Once you are in that position of advantage, those endless hours of throwing drills provide a cue for your body to turn in automatically for the appropriate throw.

After mastering a number of these setups, you will be surprised at how effortlessly you find yourself getting in for throws that come automatically. The judoka, like the jazz improvisationalist, learns through the brain and through the body a number of sequences that ripple off in performance simultaneously on demand as a prearranged set of possibilities, though not necessarily in any prearranged order. This creates a surprise for both the performer and the audience.

Setups can be used to get into a favorable throwing position from various gripping situations. Of course, the setup is often the grip. Also, you can use setups to maneuver yourself or your opponent to the head of the triangle.

INDUCING A REACTION

The principle of judo is to use the opponent's own force against him. In modern judo, the principle of action–reaction is often overlooked by coaches and instructors, but I can assure you it is just as important in modern competition as it was in the past. Today it is applied in more subtle ways. The action of rotating uke's shoulders so that he automatically moves his feet to get back to a more natural position, the action of adjusting your grip so that uke adjusts his grip, and a simple head fake in which you turn your head one way and attack in the other—all fall under the heading of action–reaction.

At higher levels of competition, the straight push–pull setup is seldom seen. It has been replaced by these more subtle maneuvers. Here are some subtle ways to entice your opponent to move in the direction or manner in which you want him to move.

CIRCLING

When I opened a dojo of my own, one of the many tasks facing me was to decide on a name for it. I wanted the dojo's name to reflect the contribution my dojo would make to its students and society. I finally decided to call it the Full Circle Judo Club. In the complete cycle of judo, a judoka becomes a student; then a sempi, or senior; and finally a sensei, teaching students, thus completing the full circle. Teaching a student to become a teacher is, in my opinion, the greatest benefit a dojo can make to society.

There was a second reason for my using the name Full Circle Judo Club. I believe that the strongest movements in judo are those of a circular action. You use circular movements to position yourself before you take a grip and as you're fighting for your grip. You will see a circle or arc in all judo throws and grappling moves. The circle or arc might not always be immediately evident, but it's there. In front throws such as tomoe nage and seoi nage, the head over heels is evident (along the axis from front to back or back to front). Sometimes the rotation is on a sideways axis from left to right or right to left, with uke's feet and head as points on the axis as uke rolls diagonally off tori's hips in throws such as haraigoshi or uchimata. In this case, the circle is less evident, but it is still there. If you watch the shoulders and hips of uke, you will always see them rotate.

The art of circling can put speed into your gripping and attacking. Top judoka use the circling action to aid in the kuzushi, or off-balancing, of their opponent as well as to maneuver themselves into good tai sabaki, or body position. The trick is to maneuver uke into moving on the outside of the circle the two of you make as you are moving around the mat. With the appropriate circling action, tori can dramatically lessen the distance and movement required for applying gripping and attacking skills.

At seminars I often demonstrate this point by tying two or three belts together and making an outline of a small circle on the mat. I then pick the fastest judoka on the mat and challenge him to a race around the circle. When the challenge is accepted, I simply stand in the middle of the circle with uke starting outside the circle. Obviously, it is no great athletic feat for me to win the race, but it is a great reminder that strategically it is always better to make your opponent circle around you rather than vice versa. This is a key principle when setting up your opponents for a throw: The more rotational speed you can generate, the more effective the attack will be.

The circular motion of judo is the foundation of all throws, pins, armlocks, and chokes. Circling step patterns are instrumental to obtaining a preferred grip. Furthermore, circling is a key principle in setting up your opponent for a throw. The more speed you can generate by circling, the more effective the attack will be. The smaller the circle you use, the more speed your rotation will have. By using the momentum of uke's larger circling action, you will add speed and power to your attack. Tori can use the momentum created by uke's larger circle to create an unstable position for uke. This unstable position, or kuzushi, is a vital concept because without kuzushi, a throw is not judo; it is merely weightlifting.

While circling your opponent (or rather, enticing your opponent to circle) and applying pressure so as to rotate uke's shoulders, do so with a down-and-out move with the wrist of your hand (figure 5.1). Your arm must be bent, and the pressure must be directed down and out. As you apply pressure to uke's shoulder, keep your lead foot pointing in the direction in which you are moving. Your lead foot must be to the outside of uke's foot. Often, uke will attack or regrip when he feels this pressure on his shoulder. This creates a good opportunity for you to attack or counterattack uke.

a

b

Figure 5.1   Circling the opponent: *(a)* tori applies pressure to rotate uke's shoulders; *(b)* tori's lead foot points in the direction he is moving and is outside uke's foot.

Often, circling is considered solely a part of the entry, but this underestimates the contribution that the act of making your opponent circle you contributes to the tactical elements in the fight. By manipulating uke's shoulders so that uke's upper body faces a slightly different angle than his lower body, you can dramatically reduce uke's ability to use his power and strength in the attack. You can also then manipulate the direction in which uke moves so as to square up his stance as he finds his position uncomfortable. With a little practice manipulating the angle of uke's shoulders, you can even maneuver uke onto the red safety mat, forcing him to fight to stay within the boundary (figure 5.2). This puts uke into an undesirable tactical position by splitting his focus between avoiding a penalty by stepping out of bounds and defending himself from your attack.

Circling your opponent to get him to step in the direction you intend to throw makes your entry easier because your entry into the throw works in unison with the momentum generated by both you and your opponent. This tai sabaki, or body positioning, is crucial for a fast, efficient attack. The more entries you have to throws that are similar, the easier it becomes to circle uke into a vulnerable situation.

Figure 5.2 With practice, you will be able to pressure uke onto the red safety mat, forcing her to fight to stay in bounds.

ENTRIES

Although we all have our favorite times and paths by which to enter into a throw, the subject of specific entries is often brushed aside in the study of competitive judo. Judoka often barrel into a throw without thought of entry or timing. This becomes obvious when on some occasions a throw produces a spectacular ippon, and sometimes the same judoka ends up on his face (or worse, on his back) on the wrong end of a counter. Often, only when a competitor specializes in one throw does he become aware of the subtleties, variations, and differences of particular entries. Thus, an uchimata expert will have a number of stepping patterns, or entries, specific for uchimata.

If you have the appropriate varied entries to each throw, you multiply your attacking opportunities fourfold by either stepping away, stepping in, stepping diagonally toward your pulling hand, or stepping diagonally toward your lifting hand (the one holding uke's collar).

Note that with each different entry, the intended direction of the completed throw must be changed. Thus, in the case of the stepping-away entry for taiotoshi, uke is thrown to tori's left front corner. During the stepping-in entry for taiotoshi, uke is thrown to tori's closer right-hand corner.

Stepping Away

The stepping-away entries are the most stable and secure entries in judo. The technique is sometimes referred to as *pulling on entry* as uke steps toward tori (figure 5.3a). Tori steps back (figure 5.3b) and uses uke's forward momentum to assist with putting uke onto tori's back (figure 5.3c). The forward momentum created by uke's pushing and tori's pulling makes this entry effective and difficult to counter. If the throw fails, tori ends up on his face rather than on his back.

In a right-hand stance in an ayotsu situation, tori steps back with his left foot when uke advances with the right foot. At the same time, tori pulls with the left hand, shifting uke's weight onto uke's right foot and allowing a strong attack from tori.

In a forward throw you must take a large step back to ensure that you have sufficient space to rotate your body in order to throw uke at least to your front corner. Otherwise you risk being countered to the back corner.

a   *b*   *c*

Figure 5.3   Stepping away entry: *(a)* uke steps toward tori; *(b)* tori steps back; *(c)* tori uses uke's forward momentum to pull uke onto tori's back.

Fine point: Try to keep the thumb of your hand holding uke's collar in front of your shoulder throughout the rotation.

Stepping In

The stepping-in entry provides two directions from which to attack. As uke backs away, tori may apply a direct attack, throwing uke straight back (figure 5.4). As uke steps back, tori steps in and spins around to face in the same direction as uke to apply a forward throw (figure 5.5). Both versions of the stepping-in entry have a higher risk of being countered than the stepping-away entry does. The very nature of tori's moving toward uke makes tori less stable. Having said that, this technique is probably the most common entry used in judo, if you include variations of uke retreating to the two back corners.

Figure 5.4   Stepping in entry, first version. Tori applies a direct attack as uke backs away.

a   *b*   *c*

Figure 5.5   Stepping in entry, second version: *(a)* uke steps back; *(b)* tori steps in and spins; *(c)* tori applies a forward throw.

Fine point: When stepping in toward uke, step diagonally with your advancing foot. For example, for a right-hand attack, step your right foot toe-to-toe with uke's right foot.

Before attacking forward with a stepping-in entry, break uke's balance by rotating his shoulder in a different direction than the direction in which his feet are pointing.

Sideways Entries

For the ease of explanation, I describe sideways entries in two separate directions: uke moving toward tori's sleeve hand and uke moving toward tori's lapel hand.

When uke is moving toward tori's sleeve hand, uke steps diagonally toward tori's sleeve as he take a right-handed sleeve lapel grip (figure 5.6a). Tori quickly turns his left foot, toes pointing out on tori's left side. This opens tori's hips, enabling him to step across between himself and uke (figure 5.6b) and apply an attack either to the front or to the rear (figure 5.6c). Be sure to turn your leading foot in the direction in which uke is moving.

a   b   c

Figure 5.6   Sideways entry, uke moving toward tori's sleeve hand: *(a)* uke steps toward tori's sleeve and takes a right-handed sleeve lapel grip; *(b)* tori opens his hips and steps between himself and uke, attacking either to the front or the rear; *(c)* tori completes the throw.

> **Fine point:** Obviously, uke made a tactical error by stepping toward tori's sleeve, but this error often occurs at the edge of the mat.

In the second situation, uke moves toward tori's right hand, which is holding uke's collar (figure 5.7a). As uke moves diagonally, tori tucks in his elbow and chin and spins his left leg in a backward semicircle (figure 5.7b). The extent of this semicircular movement depends on whether tori is attacking to the front (figure 5.7c) or back. Both movements can be effective. Great care must be taken in applying this technique because there is a high risk of being countered if uke's horizontal momentum is not redirected. A common mistake is to try to stop uke's movement and then restart it in another direction.

a   b   c

Figure 5.7 Sideways entry, uke moving toward tori's right hand on uke's collar: *(a)* tori tucks his elbow and chin; *(b)* tori spins his left leg in a backward semicircle; *(c)* tori completes the throw.

Fine point: The trick of this movement is to allow uke's momentum to move past you. Then you can assist the original movement and redirect it.

TIMING

Now let's move from body positioning to timing. The successful application of an entry to a throw relies equally on body positioning between yourself and uke, the off-balancing (which is created by the combination of tori's and uke's body movements), and the moment when tori applies the throw or takedown.

A farmer built a fence and happened to place a fencepost directly beside a rabbit hole. The rabbit stuck its head out of the hole and panicked at the sight of the farmer. While fleeing, the rabbit ran directly into the fencepost, knocking itself out. The farmer quickly picked up the rabbit and took it home for supper. He relayed the story to a friend. They then decided that this would be a great way to hunt rabbits, so the farmers put fenceposts beside every rabbit hole they could find. Of course, the first incident with the rabbit was a fluke. The farmers were never lucky enough to have this coincidental combination of timing and opportunity occur again.

Judoka who do not recognize and then train for the appropriate time at which to attack an opponent are like the farmers in this story—they are hoping that the combination of their own and uke's movements will coincide as they attack.

• **Controlling the shoulders.** To control uke's shoulders (figure 5.8), apply pressure to uke's shoulder so that both of uke's shoulders are not square with his hips. This puts uke in an unstable position, forcing him to move in the desired direction so as to regain his posture. At this moment, tori attacks using uke's momentum.

• **Changing the grip.** In a kenkayotsu situation, either tori or uke has a double lapel grip. If uke has the preferred position of holding your arm over or under his own arm (figure 5.9a), you must change

Figure 5.8   Shoulder control.

your collar grip to a grip uke does not like (figure 5.9b). As uke changes back, use that movement to your advantage (figure 5.9c). Take care that uke does not use your regripping action against you! Just before you switch your grip or before you take a small half step back as you switch the grip, give a sharp tug on uke's lapel, one sufficient to make uke's head bob slightly.

a   *b*   *c*

Figure 5.9   Grip change: *(a)* uke has the preferred position; *(b)* tori changes his collar grip to one uke doesn't like; *(c)* when uke adjusts his grip, tori takes advantage.

• **Using the head fake.** Faking left and attacking right is a trick usually used by seoi nage specialists, but it will work in many other situations. The phrase *head fake* is a little misleading. Although the head movement is the most noticed part of this trick, there is much more to it. You must turn your shoulders and hips to make uke believe you are attacking the left side (figure 5.10a). As you switch to attack the right side, lift your right foot high and step between uke's body and your own as you pivot on your left foot to attack uke's right side (figure 5.10b).

a *b*

Figure 5.10 Head fake: *(a)* tori fakes to the left; *(b)* tori attacks to the right.

• **Faking with one throw to complete another throw.** This trick could fall under the category of combination techniques (discussed in the next section), but it also falls under setups or fakes as well as meeting the criteria for demonstrating the principle of action–reaction. In this move, there is no real attempt to throw with the first throw. Threatening a throw, rather than attempting a throw, induces uke to move.

Other common throws can be used as fake combinations: seoi nage to kouchigari; osotogari to sasiashi; uchimata to kosotogake; and hizaguruma to osotogari.

COMBINATION TECHNIQUES

Combination techniques often demonstrate some of the principles of judo: throwing the opponent in the direction he chooses to go and using uke's own power against him while needing relatively little of your own power to complete the throw.

Combination techniques fall into two main categories: throws that induce the principle of action–reaction and throws that start the opponent going in one direction then are followed up with a second throw that goes in the same direction.

Action–Reaction Throws

In throws that induce the principle of action–reaction, you attack in one direction. Then, as uke pulls or pushes in the opposite direction to avoid being thrown, you apply a second throw in the direction in which uke pushed or pulled.

These types of throws can be done in two main directions. The first direction is forward to backward. Begin by attacking forward and then switch to a backward attack. Put in a strong forward attack (figure 5.11a), ensuring the

a   b

Figure 5.11 Forward to backward action–reaction combination technique: *(a)* tori attacks forward; *(b)* uke responds strongly; *(c)* tori makes a semicircle with her right foot; *(d)* tori applies a backward attack on uke's leg.

use of a lot of arm pull so that uke must respond strongly. Usually uke will retract his hips and pull backward to stop his forward momentum (figure 5.11b). As you feel uke's reaction, draw a small semicircle with the big toe of your right foot (figure 5.11c) and take a small hop with your left foot so that your body and uke's body make a T. Then, depending on your position, apply a backward attack on uke's closer leg (figure 5.11d).

The most common backward attacks are ouchigari and kouchigari. Sometimes, depending on the relation of your body position to uke's body position, hooking to the outside with either osotogari or kosotogari is appropriate.

Fine point: With the second attack, as with all backward attacks, keep your belt lower than uke's belt and your thumb in front of your shoulder as you apply the throw.

A judoka in his first combination technique training session may attempt the second throw too soon. If tori has anticipated uke's response and attacked before uke has reacted to the first attack, this often ends badly for tori. As with counters, a judoka must develop a feel for uke's movement so that the second throw becomes instinctual more than prearranged. With time and proper training, most judoka can develop this instinct.

c

d

The second direction is backward to forward. Tori applies a backward attack (figure 5.12a). To avoid being thrown backward, uke responds by moving forward (figure 5.12b). Tori then attacks with a forward throw (figure 5.12c). Immediately after uke steps off tori's initial backward attack, uke automatically steps to regain his original right or left stance. At this moment, tori attacks with a forward throw using uke's own momentum.

When applying the forward attack, apply a stepping-in entry. If you use a stepping-away entry, uke will feel the forward pull and retract his hips. This makes a forward throw difficult.

a   *b*   *c*

Figure 5.12   Backward to forward action–reaction combination technique: *(a)* tori applies a backward attack; *(b)* uke moves forward in response to the backward attack; *(c)* tori attacks with a forward throw, using uke's own momentum.

Same Direction Throws

The second category of combinations are throws in which tori starts to make uke go in one direction, then follows up with a second throw, throwing in the same direction.

Begin by attacking uke with a backward throw such as ouchigari (figure 5.13a). As uke steps off, immediately put your right foot down and take a small step with your left foot so as to deepen your foot position toward uke (figure 5.13b). Apply a second backward throw such as kouchigari or osotogari (figure 5.13c).

a   b   c

Figure 5.13   Same direction throws combination technique: *(a)* tori attacks with the backward throw ouchigari; *(b)* when uke steps off, tori puts his right foot down and steps with his left foot; *(c)* tori applies the second backward throw.

Often tori tries to apply the second throw without adjusting his distance, resulting in a failed attempt, or worse, tori being countered. Tori must take the time to adjust his body position before applying the second attack.

It is possible to morph a technique. If you attack with one throw only, at midpoint you may feel that uke has stopped the throw by strong resistance or a movement in a particular direction. At that moment, instead of retreating completely out of the throw and risking a counter, simply hop on your support foot and change the throw by changing the direction in which you intend to throw uke. Throws that work well in this situation are hooking throws such as osotogari to haraigoshi and ouchigari to uchimata.

Fine point: Keep continuous control over uke's shoulders to avoid being countered as you change the direction of the throw.

BLOCKS AND STUMBLES

This setup category is often overlooked. I intentionally call these techniques *skills* because they constitute trainable actions that produce desired and predictable outcomes. Almost all top fighters use them, but they mostly go unnoticed or are considered failed or poor attempts at traditional throws. This is because most blocks or stumble techniques are traditional throws done to the wrong leg and used to square up the opponent.

Wrong-Sided Taiotoshi

This block is used to square up an opponent who is standing in an extreme kenkayotsu gripping situation. You have a one lapel grip, uke has a grip on your lapel, and you both are attempting to get a sleeve grip (figure 5.14a). This is a common neutral situation during a fight.

From a right-handed stance, take your left hand and grab the end of uke's sleeve (the arm uke is using to hold your lapel; figure 5.14b) as you swing your left foot back in a semicircle and pivot on your right foot (figure 5.14c). Once the rotation is complete, step your right foot across in front of uke's near foot to apply a taiotoshi movement with your feet (figure 5.14d). Swing uke's body around in a semicircle so that he must step out with his retreated foot to maintain his balance (figure 5.14e). This movement squares the stance. At this point, uke's weight will be forward and his body will be bent. As uke straightens to regain his posture, step in with your left foot, making a triangle with uke's two feet and your left foot.

Be patient. Don't attack too soon with the second throw. Wait for uke to adjust his posture and balance. If you don't, you will be throwing in one direction and uke will still be moving in the other direction.

a   b

Figure 5.14   Wrong-sided taiotoshi: *(a)* uke stands in an extreme kenkayotsu gripping position and tori has a one lapel grip; *(b)* tori grabs the end of uke's sleeve; *(c)* tori and swings his left foot back, pivoting on his right foot; *(d)* tori applies a taiotoshi movment; *(e)* tori swings uke's body so uke has to step out.

c

d

e

Fine point: As you apply the stumble and swing uke's body around, keep your right thumb in front of your right shoulder so that you are pushing uke's shoulder and upper arm with your forearm.

Figure 5.15   Option A: tori attacks with a left-handed throw.

At this point you have two options. In option A, you attack with a left-handed throw such as seoi nage or sotomakikomi (figure 5.15). You can attack with an extremely strong version of drop seoi nage by simply continuing to hold the end of uke's sleeve as you apply the throw.

In option B, maintain your right-handed grip but replace your right-handed lapel grip with a back or collar grip and apply a right-handed throw such as ouchigari, kouchigari, uchimata, sumiotoshi, or a leg pick (figure 5.16). Note that because of the limited control over uke's right shoulder with option B, it is often difficult to throw for ippon with some of these suggested throws. However, it is very possible to get lower scores from this grip.

a   *b*

Figure 5.16   Option B: *(a)* tori switches to a back or collar grip; *(b)* tori applies a right-handed throw.

Wrong-Sided Sasiashi (Ankle Block)

This version is very effective in both judo and sombo when the opponent is in a crouched position.

From a kenkayotsu lapel grip, simply reach up with your right hand and grab uke's right lapel at the top of his shoulder while maintaining your original grip with your left hand (figure 5.17a). Then, with a snapping wavelike action of your wrists, pull uke's shoulders over and past uke's advanced right foot (figure 5.17b). Take a small half step forward with your right foot. With your right foot, apply a blocking movement to uke's advanced left foot (figure 5.17c). The blocking action is similar to that in sasiashi. This blocking action should make uke step forward with his left foot, squaring up uke's stance.

a   b   c

Figure 5.17 Wrong-sided sasiaski (ankle block): *(a)* from a kenkayotsu lapel grip, tori grabs uke's right lapel with his right hand; *(b)* tori pulls uke's shoulders past uke's forward foot; *(c)* tori uses his right foot to block uke's right foot.

Again, timing is critical. Do not rush your response. Wait for uke to try to regain his posture; then use the uprighting momentum against him. When uke tries to regain his balance, apply a throw such as a foot sweep, leg pick, or kata guruma, or change your grip and apply sotomakikomi.

Fine point: Note that the pulling of uke's lapel is not one of power. It is just a flick, just enough to make uke stumble, and it should be applied as you take the small half step. The half step should be more of a small stomping of your foot to create momentum.

6

Transitioning From Standing to Groundwork

Many judoka do not believe that grappling techniques will help them win matches. However, if your opponent is intimidated by your skill on the ground, this has both a psychological and a physiological effect on his fighting style. Often such opponents fight much more defensively, and their attacks are not as committed or as frequent as they might be for fear of being knocked down. This puts them in a vulnerable position. Judoka with less athletic prowess can obtain much faster results by concentrating on transitions and groundwork skills as opposed to focusing on throwing techniques.

I contend that grappling techniques are often mistrained. Most training for groundwork is done exclusively from the ground in a randori fashion, with little or no thought as to the importance of the control that should be maintained during the transition from standing to groundwork. This error is compounded by training in randori under time restraints that do not coincide with the rules of modern-day judo. It is not efficient to allow judoka to train at too slow a pace or, even worse, to allow the partner to waste valuable training time lying beneath tori and hanging on for 3 or 4 minutes just so uke can say he was not pinned. At almost every major competition, you will see a club newaza randori champion beaten on the ground by a judoka who is trained well in controlling the transition from standing to groundwork, while the champion's clubmates look on in disbelief.

Soon after competitive judoka learn the basics of newaza, they must study which throws or takedowns lead directly to which hold-downs or grappling techniques. The key to winning on the ground is not how good you can perform groundwork in a randori situation, but how effectively you can transfer standing control into ground control so that you land in an advantageous situation for applying ground techniques.

In 1993 my wife, Tracy Angus (formerly Tracy Down), was invited to compete at the World Kabudo Grappling Championships. Tracy was new to grappling but had had a very strong competitive career in judo having competed in seven world judo championships. Most of her competitive successes had come from groundwork. We decided on a tactical plan that built on her strengths: limit standing techniques to those that would leave Tracy landing flat, face to face, on her opponent or that would throw her opponent facedown with Tracy landing on her opponent's back.

To achieve this dominant position, we would have to eliminate any throw that would expose Tracy's back or put her at risk of throwing her opponent with such force that after the opponent landed on her back, the momentum would allow uke to continue rolling so that Tracy would end up at the bottom. We included throws such as ouchigari, foot sweeps, leg picks, close sasae ashi, and shallow taiotoshi. We eliminated uchimata, osotogari, and shoulder throws. All the throws or takedowns chosen for inclusion would cause the opponent to land on her belly or flat on her back with Tracy landing flat on

© David Finch/Judo Photos Unlimited

Tracy Angus of New Zealand blocks the attack of three-time World Champion Bridget Deydier of France and then follows up with a fast transition into newaza.

her opponent chest to chest. This established a dominance in the transitions that reduced Tracy's exposure to many of the unknown techniques of her unknown opponents with their unknown styles.

Our match plan was to select throws based only on their effectiveness of transition into groundwork. Once Tracy was in her dominant position, she could fight her strength, which was submission moves during groundwork. Tracy won all her matches by submission and became world kabudo grappling champion. She later went on to win yet another professional grappling tournament.

Tracy's match plan was designed specifically for the rules governing submission grappling, in which throws and takedowns are not scored heavily.

You can design your own match plan pertaining to the rules and scoring system (unlike grappling) of judo. In the rest of this chapter, I present some of the most efficient paths to follow when going from throws and takedowns to ground techniques. IJF rules are designed to ensure that the transition from standing techniques to ground techniques are skillful and immediate. This requirement significantly changed the strategy of applying groundwork techniques by streamlining the attacks.

TRANSITIONS

A fighter's goal should be to achieve the most direct route by which to take the opponent to the ground. This involves limiting the space between the thrower's body and the opponent's body, while controlling the opponent's shoulders.

The following throws and hold-downs are paired in the most direct line for the transition from that particular throw to that particular hold-down. I suggest training the transitions from standing to groundwork in two forms: first, during all randori sessions, as you throw uke, follow up with 5 to 10 seconds of newaza; second, try the transition drills suggested.

Taiotoshi Into Kesa Gatame

The control over uke's shoulders, combined with the close proximity of tori to uke's chest, makes kesa gatame an effective hold to transition into.

Apply taiotoshi in a conventional way (figure 6.1). Once you have thrown uke, continue rotating your body and follow uke to the ground to apply kesa gatame.

a

b

c

Figure 6.1 Taiotoshi into kesa gatame: *(a)* tori throws uke; *(b)* tori follows uke to the ground; *(c)* tori applies kesa gatame.

Fine point: Throughout the entire application of this technique, you must control uke's chest and shoulders by maintaining contact against uke's chest with your entire forearm.

To drill this transition, apply the skill as described but with uke starting on his knees. Once you control uke by kesa gatame, uke then applies an appropriate escape technique. After tori has rolled off uke, tori does a given number of push-ups. Meanwhile, uke stands up in preparation for reversing the roles. Adapt reps and sets to suit the energy system you wish to train.

Osotogari Into Kesa Gatame

Apply osotogari in the normal fashion, ensuring that you have firm chest contact throughout the throw and during the transition into kesa gatame (figure 6.2). Tori must lift uke high enough during the throwing action so that uke can do a safe break fall.

a   *b*

Figure 6.2   Osotogari into kesa gatame: *(a)* tori applies osotogari as usual; *(b)* uke does a safe break fall.

> **Fine point:** In a right-handed throw, be sure to pull your right hand into the right side of your body during the completion of the throw. This will ensure control over uke's shoulders in preparation for the hold-down.

To drill the transition, execute it as previously described, except uke should be kneeling on one knee with the other leg up on one foot.

Leg Pick Into Yokoshiho Gatame

Apply a leg pick in a traditional manner, ensuring that you have firm head-to-chest contact with uke (figure 6.3). Finish the pick with a kosotogake-type hooking action; then pull yourself directly into yokoshiho gatame.

a

b

Figure 6.3   Leg pick into yokoshiho gatame: *(a)* tori applies a leg pick as usual; *(b)* tori ends the pick with a kosotagake hooking action; *(c)* tori moves immediately into yokoshiho gatame.

c

> **Fine point:** Immediately after landing, secure control over uke's shoulders by pulling in with your lapel grip. Let go of uke's leg and grab the skirt of uke's gi from under the upper hamstring of uke's other leg.

To drill the transition, follow the same procedure as with the osotogari into kesa gatame transition.

Sumi Gaeshi Into Tateshiho Gatame

Apply sumi gaeshi in a normal fashion, being sure to control uke's upper body as you roll with him (figure 6.4). Let go of his sleeve and cup the triceps of that same arm while applying a strong pulling action on his belt. You must then roll immediately over your shoulder straight into tateshiho gatame while maintaining a solid grip on uke's belt.

a

b

Figure 6.4   Sumi gaeshi into tateshiho gatame: *(a)* tori applies sumi gaeshi as usual; *(b)* tori grabs uke's arm and pulls strongly on his belt; *(c)* tori rolls over into tateshiho gatame.

c

Fine point: Do not roll straight back over your head because it would be difficult to complete the roll. Instead, roll over the shoulder that is holding uke's belt.

To drill the transition, do shadow uchikomi, concentrating on a fast fluid rolling action over the appropriate shoulder.

Kouchigari Into Kesa Gatame

Apply kouchigari in a normal fashion, being sure to maintain control over uke's shoulders especially once he has hit the ground (figure 6.5). Achieve this control by rotating your wrist so as to land with your sleeve hand pinning uke's arm to the mat. Pin uke's other shoulder to the mat with your forearm and then pass over uke's outstretched leg and into kesa gatame.

a

b

c

Figure 6.5 Kouchigari into kesa gatame: *(a)* tori applies kouchigari as usual; *(b)* tori pins uke's shoulder to the mat; *(c)* tori moves over uke's outstretched leg into kesa gatame.

Fine point: While passing over uke's outstretched leg during a right-handed throw, bend down on your right knee and momentarily trap that leg between your bent knee and foot as you bring your left leg over uke's outstretched knee.

WRONG-SIDED THROWS

Although all top fighters look for a opportunity to throw their opponents for full ippon, sometimes it becomes necessary to take an opponent skillfully to the ground for an opportunity at groundwork. (Note: It is illegal to drag an opponent to the ground, but it is legal to throw an opponent in a skillful manner onto his belly and then enter into groundwork.)

As well as being good setups for throws, the wrong-sided taiotoshi and sasiashi create sound opportunities to fling uke onto his belly. Do the block (figure 6.6a) as described in chapter 5 under the heading "Blocks and

a

b

c

d

Figure 6.6   Wrong-sided throw: *(a)* tori blocks uke; *(b)* when uke steps to square up, tori steps back; *(c)* tori flicks uke with both hands to put him off balance; *(d)* tori finishes with newaza.

Stumbles" (page 97). Once uke takes a step to square up, immediately step back with your right leg instead of forward (figure 6.6b). With both hands, give uke another flick in a wavelike action without giving uke time to regain his posture (figure 6.6c). When uke lands on the mat, keep hold of his lapel and follow up immediately with newaza (figure 6.6d).

ARMLOCK TRANSITIONS INTO NEWAZA

Another sound way to take someone down into newaza is by using a standing armlock. Standing armlocks were very popular in competition until throwing from a standing armlock such as wakigatame was deemed illegal. With this change, wakigatame became a risky standing armlock to try because, if you lost control on the way to the ground, it would be deemed an attempted throw and you would be severely penalized. It is unfortunate that the popularity of all standing armlocks went down, even though in reality the success rate of standing armlocks is quite low. If I had to guess, I would say that maybe 1 out of 10 or fewer standing armlocks are successful. But with such ease of application, there are a number of aspects that make attempting a standing armlock valuable.

Standing armlocks still have three valuable tactical applications:

1. There is always the chance of obtaining ippon.
2. To avoid the standing armlock, often uke would do a forward roll, putting him at a disadvantage by allowing tori to follow up on the ground.
3. There is a significant intimidation factor when it comes to gripping. If your opponent gripped behind your collar and you almost caught him in an armlock, this would make him second-guess the application of the same grip a second time.

The standing armlock has other important benefits as well, particularly ude garame. Armlocks are easy to apply safely, and they carry little danger of being countered or penalized for false attack. Also, ude garame is often applied when uke has a high collar grip. Believe me, as I have indicated already, if you are even coming close to catching uke with a standing armlock, it slows down his enthusiasm for reaching up again over your shoulder for a collar grip.

The two most important defenses for avoiding being armlocked are retracting your arm and doing a forward roll out of the armlock. Option 1 gets rid of a potentially dangerous grip from uke. With option 2, you have a great opportunity to follow up in newaza. As you can see, the standing armlock is well worth a second look.

Ude Garame As a Transition Into Newaza

Although other standing armlocks can be applied, ude garame lends itself best to the transition to newaza. In this version, uke has a sleeve collar grip (figure 6.7a). Tori first creates tension on uke's arm by pushing on uke's shoulder just above uke's armpit (figure 6.7b). It is not necessary for uke's arm to be completely straight. As tori presses on uke's shoulder, tori pulls up his shoulder while bringing down his ear so as to create a V shape with his neck in which to trap uke's wrist (figure 6.7c). Tori's elbow must be pointing up at this moment of the move. Tori maintains pressure on uke's chest as tori reaches over with his free left hand and cups uke's elbow, ensuring that tori's fingers are fully around and under uke's elbow joint. As this action is taking place, tori takes a small step, circling toward the arm that is being attacked (figure 6.7d). As uke's elbow is passing tori's face, tori takes another step, this

a

b

c

d

Figure 6.7 Ude garame into newaza: *(a)* uke is holding tori in a sleeve collar grip; *(b)* tori creates tension by pushing on uke's shoulder; *(c)* tori pushes on uke's shoulder and traps uke's wrist with his neck; *(d)* tori grabs uke's elbow with his other hand and steps toward the arm being attacked.

time with his left foot, changing the direction of force to the left and pulling uke's wrist into the V. Only now does tori take the pressure off uke's shoulder. Tori uses his free right hand to cup the elbow, and then with both hands tori pulls uke's elbow into tori's belly.

To use the second hand on the elbow, tori may erroneously let the pressure off uke's shoulder too soon. Uke's elbow should be almost straight before tori lets the pressure off uke's shoulder.

Fine point: Tori must never push uke's shoulder with a straight arm and wrist. When you create tension by pushing on uke's shoulder, bend your wrist in and push with the top or back side of the wrist.

COMBINATION GROUND TECHNIQUES

Success in groundwork often lies in being ready with a follow-up technique in case your opponent evades your first attack. In this way you double your chances. A combination of techniques is most effective for this approach. These combinations require you to anticipate the direction and movement of the opponent's avoidance of your first attack.

The following setups for armlocks and chokes take advantage of uke's movements as he tries to avoid or escape from a given hold-down. (These hold-downs were discussed in chapter 4.)

First it is important to realize that the secret of holding uke down is to rest your body weight on uke's body, almost snuggling up to him (figure 6.8a). For uke to escape, he must lift either a shoulder or a hip to create space to bridge you over or to twist out. As uke's hips come up, you know one of his shoulders must follow to create a twisting movement. As you feel uke's shoulder start to rise, smother it by applying more of your weight to that shoulder (figure 6.8b). The natural reaction for uke now is to lift the other shoulder. As you feel uke start to do this, simply adjust your hips and put more weight on the offending shoulder. This ability to selectively pinpoint the use of your power and control is useful in all aspects of judo.

There are an endless number of combinations from one ground move to another. Here are some of the more common ones. These moves will give you the foundation to develop your favorite combinations and the ability to improvise further combinations as needed.

Circle of Hold-Down

A judoka attempting to be proficient in newaza must be able to anticipate his opponent's moves and adjust to them before the attack gains momentum. A great way to develop this ability to anticipate uke's movement is to do the classic circle of hold-down drill. The purpose of the drill is to develop a smooth transition from one technique to another by reading the body movement

a

b

Figure 6.8 *(a)* To hold uke down, rest your body weight on him. *(b)* If he tries to escape by lifting a shoulder, apply more pressure to that shoulder.

of your opponent. As with all drills, the spirit of the drill must be respected. Uke's and tori's resistance must be at a level so as to foster continual learning and development.

In phase 1, uke is on his hands and knees (figure 6.9a). Tori puts his hand behind his own back and places his chest on uke's back. With both legs spread, tori circles around uke's tucked body.

In phase 2, uke is on his knees with his arms spread out (figure 6.9b). Tori is in the same position and has the same job, but now he has the added job of maneuvering over uke's outstretched arms. At no time should tori take his weight off uke, but the pressure may come from different sides of tori's chest as he moves.

In phase 3, uke is lying on his back (figure 6.9c). Tori starts with kesa gatame, moves to kata gatame, then to kamishiho gatame, and then to yokoshiho gatame and tateshiho gatame. Tori must control the appropriate shoulder before completely switching from one move to the next.

For phase 4, repeat the drill, but this time have uke move in a prearranged pattern to simulate an escape attempt (figure 6.9d). Tori switches techniques at the appropriate time. Do not rush this phase of the drill. Relax and try to get a real sense or feel for uke's body. Get a sense of uke's kinetic chain during his movement.

For example, for uke to turn his shoulder in toward you, his heel has to come into his buttocks, his hips must rise, his head must face you, his hips and trunk must move ahead of his shoulder, and then finally his shoulder

a

b

c

d

Figure 6.9 Circle of hold-down: *(a)* phase 1, tori circles around uke's tucked body; *(b)* phase 2, tori moves over uke's outstretched arms; *(c)* phase 3, tori controls the appropriate shoulder before going to the next move; *(d)* phase 4, tori counters as uke tries to escape.

can rise. Once you understand this kinetic chain, you will feel instinctively that the beginning of the shoulder rising is in fact uke's heel coming toward his buttocks so that uke can bridge. When you can recognize the kinetic chain of movement, it will be easier to stay one step ahead of uke. The feeling for movement from a hold to an appropriate armlock or choke would be the same. Training your body to understand, follow, and anticipate this kinetic chain is the real value of this drill, which achieves more than the slavish imitation of "when uke turns this way, you apply this holding technique."

For phase 5, uke starts on his back and is free to try to escape in any legal fashion. Tori must try to read uke's movement and adjust by changing positions or holds.

Kesa Gatame to Koshi-Jimi

Consider a situation in which you are applying kesa gatame and uke is escaping by turning away from you (figure 6.10a). Once uke gets to the point of no return, grab uke's right lapel and pull it down toward uke's belt. With your left hand, reach under uke's chin and apply koshi-jimi (figure 6.10b).

a

b

Figure 6.10 Kesa gatame to koshi-jimi: *(a)* uke turns away from tori to escape; *(b)* tori applies koshi-jimi.

Kesa Gatame to Wakigatame

Now consider a situation in which you are applying kesa gatame and uke tries to escape by turning into you and pushing your upper body away (figure 6.11a). At this point, let go of uke's sleeve with your right hand and trap his wrist against your chest (figure 6.11b). Once you have secured uke's wrist to your chest, move in the direction that uke is pushing and pull uke onto his belly (figure 6.11c) and apply wakigatame (figure 6.11d).

a

b

c

d

Figure 6.11 Kesa gatame to wakigatame: *(a)* uke attempts to escape from kesa gatame by turning into tori and pushing him away; *(b)* tori release uke's sleeve and traps his wrist; *(c)* tori pulls uke onto his belly; *(d)* tori applies wakigatame.

Yokoshiho Gatame to Ude Gatame

Consider a situation in which you are applying yokoshiho gatame. Uke tries to escape with the shrimp movement by pulling in and pushing away with a grip over your belt or back (figure 6.12a). Maneuver so that you are at a slight angle toward uke's head or feet, depending on what side of your head uke's arm is on. Try to get your shoulder at least as high as uke's elbow on his outstretched arm. As uke pushes you away, cup uke's triceps just above the elbow joint. Make a V shape with the side of your head and shoulder and trap uke's arm (figure 6.12b). Once the arm is trapped, scoop your right hand up and in the same angle as your body position. As you bring your left hand up to uke's elbow, firmly apply ude gatame.

a

b

Figure 6.12   Yokoshiho gatame to ude gatame: *(a)* uke attempts to escape yokoshiho gatame with a shrimp movement; *(b)* tori adjusts position and traps uke's arm.

Kamishiho Gatame to Figure Four Armlock

Consider a situation in which you are applying kamishiho gatame. Your opponent tries to escape by pushing both of his hands on your one shoulder, in this case your right shoulder, and twisting his face down (figure 6.13a). Let go of uke's belt with your right arm and trap uke's arm against your chest by hooking uke's arm above the elbow (figure 6.13b). Immediately cup uke's wrist with your right hand and grab your own right wrist with your left hand, creating a figure four (figure 6.13c). Now bring your knees up and over uke's head so that you are kneeling over uke's head and uke is on his side (figure 6.13d). Apply a figure four armlock.

a

b

c

d

Figure 6.13 Kamishiho gatame to figure four armlock: (a) uke attempts to escape by pushing on tori's right shoulder and twisting his face down; (b) tori releases uke's belt and traps uke's arm; (c) tori creates a figure four by cupping uke's wrist with his left hand and grabbing his own wrist with his right hand; (d) tori kneels over uke's head and applies a figure four armlock.

REVERSALS

It is a great tactical advantage to be able to switch from being in prone (face-down) defensive position with your opponent on top of you, to an attacking position (thus reversing the situation) with you on top of your opponent. This tactic also offers a physical and psychological advantage because it inhibits the opponent's enthusiasm for attacking you on the ground.

Until the mid- to late 1980s, a judoka would train for two basic newaza competitive situations: being on top of the opponent (most often between uke's legs or on uke's back) and fighting from his own back. Even then it was considered a disadvantage to be fighting from your own back. Although many judoka specialized in this technique, they had to be better at newaza than their opponents to be effective.

Under the revised rules of judo, tori has to demonstrate immediate progression toward a pin, choke, or armlock. Once the progression stops, the referee must call matte, and the fighters must stand to start from a neutral position. Since the rule changes, it has become fairly easy for judoka who preferred tachi waza to block the progression of the traditional newaza expert who fought from his back for the short time it took to demonstrate that there was no immediate progression and thus secure a matte call.

In competition today, a high percentage of newaza exchanges arise from a failed attack in which the attacker stays facedown with arms and leg squeezed and with no intention of attacking. His plan is strictly to negate his opponent's attack long enough to get the matte call or to turn onto his back and hug his opponent's leg with the only goal a matte call.

Moreover, with no real threat of retaliation in the form of a counterattack, your opponent's attack will be stronger and more confident. So it is important that your opponent knows that you are always hunting for a score, either in groundwork or standing. Of course, it would be a grave tactical error to put yourself at risk when applying a counterattack. Think of reversals in groundwork as a two-step process to make it a useful tactic. The first step of the progression is to stop your opponent from gaining more control over the situation. The second step is for you to gain control over one of uke's limbs, most often a leg.

To apply a hold, choke, or armlock, you must have control over uke's body. If you fully control one of your opponent's limbs, it will be very difficult for your opponent to control your body. At the same time, you will have a direction in which to escape or from which to apply a counter.

Reversal 1

You begin facedown. Your opponent is attacking from the direction of your head. Most likely uke will grab your belt and collar to pull you forward. Grab uke's advanced right leg just below the knee with your left hand and seize uke's ankle with your right hand (figure 6.14a). Pull uke's leg into and across your body. After grabbing uke's leg, retract your elbows. As uke's leg buckles, crawl up uke's body, grabbing his belt with your right hand (figure 6.14b), and then control uke's shoulders and head to apply yokoshiho gatame (figure 6.14c).

As you grab uke's leg, be sure not to reach out too far and extend your arms. This would allow uke to hook your armpit and head with his legs in a sangaku-jimi action. If uke's leg is too far away, wait for uke to pull his legs forward. By using uke's pulling action, you can close the distance between uke and yourself and grab uke's leg safely. Be sure to follow up with your legs in an action similar to a frog hopping.

a

b

c

Figure 6.14 Reversal 1: *(a)* tori begins facedown; *(b)* as uke attacks from the head, tori grabs uke's right leg with his left hand and uke's ankle with his right hand, and pulls uke's leg across his body; *(c)* when uke falters, tori moves up uke's body and applies yokoshiho gatame.

Fine point: Grip uke's leg in the order given to avoid being armlocked with ashi guruma.

Reversal 2

You are in a facedown position and are being attacked with a choke. As you lie facedown, uke is on your back, attacking the right side of your neck with a choke (figure 6.15a). As soon as you feel uke on your back, bring your right knee up to your elbow, keeping your right hip in contact with the mat to prevent uke's foot and leg from hooking your right leg. Bring your right ear down to your right shoulder. Reach across your face with your left hand and meet uke's incoming hand. Grab uke's hand with your left hand (figure 6.15b). Cup under uke's elbow and push the elbow up toward the top of your head, slipping your head through the gap you created (figure 6.15c). Uke's arm is now on the left side of your head. Pull uke's arm down as you shift your body up until uke's armpit is tight against the top of your shoulder. It is relatively easy at this point just to hold uke in that position for a matte call.

a

b

c

Figure 6.15 Reversal 2: *(a)* tori begins facedown as uke attacks with a choke; *(b)* tori reaches and grabs uke's hand; *(c)* tori pushes uke's elbow up and escapes through the gap created.

Reversal 3 (a continuation of reversal 2)

If the tactical situation arises and it is appropriate to try to attack your opponent on the ground, you can simply let go of uke's arm with your left hand as you bring your left knee up (figure 6.16a). You will notice that as your leg comes up toward your head, so does uke's foot. Uke undoubtedly would have hooked on your left leg. Reach down and cup the heel of uke's foot (figure 6.16b) and clear it from your hip (figure 6.16c). Immediately pull uke's arm under your body as if you were climbing a rope hand-over-hand with your face turned to your right side until you adjust your body into a pinning position (figure 6.16d).

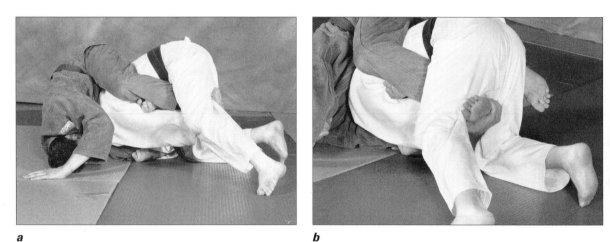

a
b

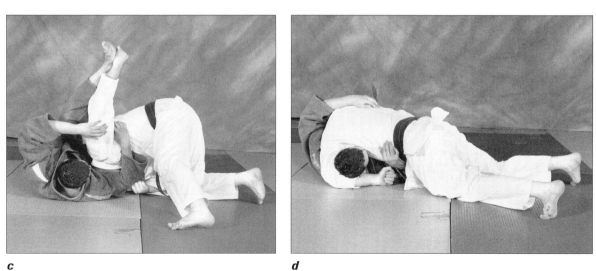

c
d

Figure 6.16 Reversal 3: *(a)* tori releases uke's arm as he raises his left knee; *(b)* tori cups uke's heel; *(c)* tori clears uke's heel from his hip; *(d)* tori pins uke.

As you try to get uke's arm to the other side of your head, often uke will try to pull your arm full over his head. Use a combination of lifting uke's arm up and driving your head through the gap created. This is a little uncomfortable, but remember that you are in a fight!

| **Fine point:** It will take determined practice to learn how to buck, twist, and maneuver your hips to put you in a pinning position, but it is well worth the study time.

LINKING ELEMENTS

So far we have looked at the techniques or skills of judo. The rest of the book will cover match strategies and the relationship of conditioning to tactics and skills. Because the requirements of competitive judo are complex and the specific activities need to be merged, it is important to understand the linking of these elements.

In the introduction, I discussed the concept of thinking of each necessary stage (from getting your grip to being awarded ippon) as a gate that you pass through to get to the next stage of the scrimmage. Linking is simply the action of going from one gate, or stage, to another. This method of learning is called the whole–part–whole method, and it is often used when learning a new move. The student sees the whole skill; then the coach breaks it down into parts. For example, a throw might be broken down into the pull, the correct body position, and the finish. The final stage would be to put all the parts together to perform the complete throw. I suggest using this method not only when learning a particular technique, but also when learning the sequence of all steps from hajimi to matte or ippon.

A judo match can be divided into a series of mastered judo skills performed in a specific order. One skill is linked to the next skill until the final outcome has been achieved—ippon is awarded or the progression toward ippon is momentarily stopped.

So far we have looked at all the skills covered as separate entities. This is a fairly common way of learning skills, and in this mode of learning the mind can grasp the principles of each skill. But in judo competition, you need a much deeper understanding of the skill. This deeper understanding is often referred to as a feel for the move; in other words, your body knows the move. Once a judoka creates the muscle memory of these individual skills, he is ready to link the skills in the order outlined in the following sequence of gates:

1. Getting the grip
2. Circling to the head of the triangle
3. Executing the throw
4. Transitioning to groundwork
5. Applying the ground skill

The drills for learning skills are combined with drills that develop judo-specific conditioning. Only when the judoka learns to link the skills in an efficient, fluid movement should this linking process be introduced as a judo conditioning tool. The training effect can be manipulated to produce the desired level of conditioning by changing the tempo or duration of the activity, adding rest periods, and increasing the opponent's resistance during the drill.

Different types of fitness must be developed in sequence throughout the year. This will be discussed in detail in part III, but for now there are some basics that must be covered. An aerobic base must be built early in the season. There are two main ways of building this base.

Long submaximal aerobic training is most commonly achieved through running or biking sessions of 20 to 40 minutes long. I strongly suggest that this type of training not be replaced by long, slow judo drills because you need to create both the muscle memory and the judo-specific conditioning for judo at or near the intensity that you will use in competition. It is my belief that it is not in the best interest of your judo to spend too much time doing judo at submaximum speed and intensity.

A second way to build the aerobic energy system is to do repeated, shorter, but more intense bouts of exercise with rest periods within a predetermined work period. In contrast to the long, slow form of training, this method does lend itself well to the complete skill-linking drills to develop skill and conditioning at the same time.

To develop different types of fitness, change the work–rest intervals and the intensity of the activity to meet the demands within the parameters of the energy system being trained that session. A word of caution: It is strongly recommended that you train the desired energy system in a conventional way during the early part of that phase by running or biking, for example. In this way, your judo skill does not suffer as you try to build a base in that energy system. The traditional training could be as long as 25 to 50 percent of the length of that training phase for that particular energy system.

For example, a drill that uses taiotoshi to develop important aspects of taiotoshi would start with tori pulling uke to the front corner. Tori uses his rotation of entry and lowers his center of balance, finishing with his hands. Performing the following drills at full speed, intensity, and duration will help you develop the skill as well as condition your body for judo. The body movements during the drills create a training effect on your body.

Here is an example of a drill sequence from a specific grip. The task of the drill is to fight with a double lapel grip. Once the grip is secured, circle to an appropriate throwing position. Use the appropriate throw (review the throws recommended for the double lapel grip in chapter 2, page 27). Take the most direct route into a groundwork skill. Stand up and repeat the complete drill. Perform six sets (six repetitions) with 3 minutes of work and 3 minutes of rest. The intensity should be 80 to 85 percent of maximum effort.

Once these drills and processes become efficient and instinctive, practice in judo-specific conditioning will combine the skills of throwing, transitioning, and using groundwork moves. Perform these drills at full speed to develop judo-specific speed. Perform them at the right duration for judo-specific endurance by combining all of these requirements for competitive judo.

7

Scouting and Analyzing the Opponent

It is an obvious advantage to have a general understanding of how your opponent has fought in the past. Scouting and analyzing your opponent will give you this inside knowledge, but be careful not to fall into the trap of concentrating on your opponent's style at the expense of your own fighting style. Also, your opponent will surely be adding to and changing his repertoire of skills, throws, and tactics on an ongoing basis.

Obviously, having a general idea of your opponent's basic strategies is useful when creating an effective match plan. For example, is your opponent right-handed or left-handed? Does he switch sides throughout the fight? What grip does he prefer, and what throws does he attempt when fighting someone who uses your fighting style?

SCOUTING METHODS

There are a number of ways to scout your opponent, including observing your opponent's matches, watching videos of previous matches, and talking to other fighters.

Personal experience, either in competition or by watching others, is invaluable. However, because you may be fighting or preparing to fight, your coach or teammates may have to watch and scout your opponent for you.

Watching videos of previous matches can be helpful. A video camera is a very useful tool! Frame-by-frame analysis can tell you a great deal.

Other fighters who have previously fought your opponent can be a very valuable resource as well. Try to get as much information on what your opponent does. A word of warning: When you design your match strategy, focus on what skills you use, not on what your friend used on your opponent. Just because your friend can throw an opponent with seoi nage does not mean that you should try seoi nage if that is not a throw you are comfortable with!

Take notes on a particular trait of your opponent's fighting style and then identify strategies to combat it. Be specific! Write down which grip you want to take hold with, which way it may be best for you to circle, and so on. To reinforce your confidence in your identification of a strategy, identify which drills would assist in your preparation. If you are not currently using drills that would help, you must design them.

Now that you understand the methods of fighting from the previous chapters, let's discuss specific questions to answer when scouting an opponent. Remember, these are only general fighting traits. Each fighter has the freedom to change his fighting style at will at any time in the match, but under pressure surprisingly few do.

Although scouting an opponent will help you prepare for the match, you also need to be flexible, able to adapt if your opponent does something unexpected.

Note that in both of the checklists in the following sections, I use the words *clue*, *might*, *indicate*, and *suggest*. There is no guarantee that because your opponent behaved in a particular manner in the past, he will behave the same way this time or next time. These scouting indicators are just ways to become aware of your opponent. Do not give them too much weight. If you change your fighting style so that you react to how your opponent fights instead of fighting in your strongest style, then you are making a grave mistake.

Drilling is crucial because it allows you to extend your style. By fighting and defending from unfamiliar grips or situations during drills, you develop a deeper understanding of that particular grip or situation even though you may never use it in a contest. As an attacker you become comfortable fighting against that grip or situation, reacting to a given situation in an appropriate way will become part of your normal fighting style. Eventually, by adding more drills and situations, you will find that slight adjustments will become natural and will not negatively affect your fighting style. New drills deepen your understanding of more and more situations so that you can then react naturally in more situations.

SCOUTING AN OPPONENT YOU DON'T KNOW

When you are fighting an unknown fighter, you can make assumptions regarding the gripping style and the throws your opponent may use. A tall fighter will probably take advantage of his height by using a sleeve collar grip or an unorthodox grip such as a one-sided sleeve back grip. The most likely throws for a tall fighter would be hooking and rotating throws such as uchimata, osotogari, and haraigoshi. Shorter fighters often use a one-handed grip or a low sleeve lapel grip, and lifting throws such as seoi nage, toemo nage, pickups, and leg picks. Of course, these are generalizations; as the match progresses, you will discover whether they fit or not. Nevertheless, such insights do give you an edge.

If your opponent is unknown to you, you must carefully watch him warm up just before the match to gather clues as to his preferred arousal level. The arousal level may tell you something about his fighting style. For example, for tori to apply a dropping throw such as seoi nage or kata guruma, both fighters must be moving and active. Such a fast tempo requires a high arousal level. However, hooking throws such as osotogari or uchimata can be applied when uke is static and bent over. Often fighters who use these throws need a slower, more controlled tempo requiring a lower arousal level.

Certain grips lend themselves to particular throws and thus indicate on which side the throw will probably be attempted. A judoka would be unlikely to attack with ippon seoi nage after bending uke over with a sleeve collar grip. The deeper you understand gripping, the better you can assess your opponent's options when you watch him fight and when you fight him.

You can gain important insights into your opponent by examining a record of throws and grappling techniques that he has used previously. In modern-day judo, coaches often keep a record of the results of their judoka's opponents, including this information. The more successful the judoka, the more coaches keep track. Interestingly, such a focus on scouting is a great incentive for champions to continually add to their repertoire of skills.

When fighting an opponent you don't know, you must read the clues your opponent provides; some of these clues can be gathered well before the match. When researching an opponent, ask the following questions:

1. Does he make fast, sharp, almost erratic movements, or are his movements calm and controlled? You can get this information by watching your opponent's mannerisms and warm-up at the side of the mat.

2. Which way does he circle to get a grip? Which foot does he lead with? This information often will provide a clue as to whether you are facing a right- or left-handed fighter.

3. What grips does he use? How much body spacing does he try to maintain? The kind of grips and the amount of space between uke's body and your own body provides much information as to which throws uke will try. Certain throws are more effective when combined with particular grips.

The space that uke tries to maintain will also give you a clue as to uke's throwing style. If your opponent tries to pull you in, closing the space, usually he will apply throws such as uchimata, haraigoshi, or sumi gaeshi. However, if your opponent tries to maintain or create space, usually he will attack with dropping throws such as seoi nage, kata guruma, and leg picks because these throws require more space between the opponents before they can be applied.

4. Where does uke apply throws? If your opponent works his way to the edge of the mat, it might indicate that he is not comfortable with groundwork. If he applies the throw square in the middle of the mat, it could be that he likes a bit of newaza.

SCOUTING AN OPPONENT YOU KNOW

Do not get complacent about scouting a known opponent, especially one you have defeated in the past. Such a mistake can cost you dearly because, just as you are trying to develop new elements to your fighting, so is your opponent. Treat old opponents just as you would unknown ones; the only difference is that you can add your own firsthand experience to your combined list of scouting techniques.

When preparing for a match against an opponent you know, research the answers to the following questions:

1. What is the opponent's match tempo? Will he come at you quickly, trying to get a one-handed grip, shake you, and then apply a leg pick or drop kata guruma when you are distracted by the shaking? Or is he a control fighter

© Empics

It is just as important to scout a familiar opponent as it is an unfamiliar one.

who will try to get a strong controlling grip, hoping either to control you to the extent that you cannot attack and get a penalty or intending to end the match with one big throw?

2. Does he fight migi (right) or hidari (left)? Your opponent's stance will undoubtedly influence the way he circles to put himself into a good throwing position.

3. Which grip does he use? The grip he uses also will affect the way you should circle to get your grip and which strategies you might need to use to ensure that you get your preferred grip.

4. What throws does he prefer to use on a right-handed opponent or on a left-handed opponent? Many fighters use different entries to the same throw depending on whether the opponent is standing right or left. Other fighters simply try different throws.

5. Does he counter, or does he ride out attacks? In general, fast-paced fighters step off or ride out throws, but control fighters will take advantage of a controlling grip and try to counter your attack. Both types of fighters may be opportunistic and try to counter a poorly executed attack.

6. Is he strong on groundwork? Notice if your opponent takes every opportunity to follow up into groundwork. Does he actively try to get you in position

to apply ground moves on you? Once he has an opponent on the ground, does he just cover up and wait for matte?

This chapter covered both ways of scouting opponents to ascertain their strengths and weaknesses and the process of identifying clues as to what the tempo of the match may be. The next chapter will cover how to combine the information you have identified or surmised and connect it to a number of factors related to your own judo preferences and abilities. You then blend that mixture first into a general match plan, and then into a more opponent-specific match plan.

8

Developing and Modifying a Match Plan

A judoka must understand not only the rules of judo but also the intent of those rules. When designing your match plan, you must ensure that it is consistent with the intent of the rules, takes into account your physical strengths and limitations, incorporates your most effective techniques, helps you set the tempo of the match, outlines body movement direction and gripping strategy, allows you to adjust tactics during the match, and includes strategies to cope with competing while injured.

CREATING THE MATCH PLAN

First, your match plan must be consistent with the intent of the rules. For example, grips and attacks, whether standing or on the ground, must show an intent to work toward a score. Use time analysis, based on a close study of the rules, to design tactics of attacking and gripping. In the rules of judo, once every 15 seconds a judoka must attack or at least be perceived to be working toward an attacking opportunity. Otherwise, the offending judoka receives a penalty.

If a judoka adopts an overly defensive posture to avoid being thrown, the offending judoka receives a penalty. As you know, not only do your opponent's penalties result in your receiving a score, but his accumulative penalty scores also increase.

Judo is a sport of many short bouts of work and rest. If you control and win each of those short work intervals, you win the match by continually (within each period) controlling the grip and tempo of the fight. Thus you can win by either using your grip to attack and score or by controlling the grip so that if you cannot attack effectively, you can force your opponent into a defensive situation so that he cannot attack effectively or at all. Either you counter your opponent's ineffective attack or your opponent receives a penalty for not attacking within the 15-second window. Either way you receive a score.

Too many fighters underestimate the effectiveness of forcing the opponent to receive penalties. A number of world and Olympic medalists have won their medals without obtaining one positive score throughout the competition. I do not recommend that this be your only goal, but it is a very effective tactic that must not be overlooked.

Evaluate both strengths and weaknesses when formulating your match plan.

Second, make sure your match play is supported by an analysis of your physical strengths and limitations. Analyze your strengths and weaknesses, both physical and technical, to help you put together a repertoire of grips, stepping patterns, and attacks for different situations. A physically strong judoka may try to control uke by breaking uke's posture by bending him over to a compromised position. A less physical judoka with a better technical base may use circling and body positioning to maneuver uke into a compromised position.

Third, base your match plan on a technique rating system. By rating the most effective skills and developing them, a judoka builds a repertoire of techniques that will be the most effective in a given situation. A sample throw-rating system was used in chapter 3. You can also use your own experiences and personal preferences to grade techniques.

Fourth, your match plan should help you decide the tempo of the match. Each particular throw and strategy is supported by a particular tempo. For example, a kata guruma or seoi nage expert prefers a fast-moving pace or tempo. Osotogari and uchimata experts do not rely as heavily on the tempo of the match as they do on body position to apply an effective attack.

You also need to consider that judo is a stop-and-start sport with work and rest intervals of varying durations and intensities. A mixture of tempo is often used, depending on the match score. Often a fast flurry is used to get the first score or to tie up a score. Slowing the pace of the match might be called for when you are winning. Slow the pace by using a more controlling grip so as to avoid an unexpected opportunistic attack from your opponent.

When choosing the appropriate tempo, the judoka must analyze the extent to which his energy systems have been prepared. A fast-paced match in which many dropping techniques such as seoi nage or kata guruma are used takes a lot more energy than a controlled fight featuring hooking throws such as osotogari or uchimata. Many judoka have been branded as out of shape when in reality an overuse of drop attacks would exhaust any fighter. The ability to change the tempo of a match and the type of throw you use is vital to implementing an effective match plan.

Fifth, your match plan should include an outline of the direction of body movement and gripping strategy. Efficient use of body movement and gripping strategies keeps you in control of the tempo of a fight and conserves energy. A true understanding of gripping and the ability to use different grips also opens up different throwing possibilities while limiting your opponent's chances to attack.

Sixth, the match plan must have a tactical basis that emphasizes the ability to adjust tactics during the match. As with all good strategies, your match plan must be flexible. The more varied your understanding of different grips and fighting styles is, the more flexible you can be.

Finally, because injuries are a part of all sports, include strategies in your match plan to support you if you are competing while injured or sick. Surprisingly,

I have found that if the injury is not too severe, often those are my best tournaments, possibly because I don't put as much pressure on myself. The ability to fight with either a right- or left-handed grip often will help protect an injury. A judoka may find it easier to hold left but still throw to his normal right side rather than try to attack on his less dominant side when compensating for an injury.

SAMPLE PLAN

In this section, I describe the process I used to map out my match plan for a recent competition. I do this not to emphasize the results but to describe the thought process.

First, I designed a goal plan, taking into consideration my immediate circumstances, my condition, my injuries, and the location of the competition. Then I designed a specific plan for each opponent that I would meet in each match. During each break in the action, I quickly evaluated the plan and then reminded myself of the plan or made small adjustments to it.

As you can see, a well-designed match plan is a combination of many factors, some of which you can control and some of which you cannot. It is imperative that you turn as many of these factors to your favor as possible. As you get more experience at designing match plans, you will be able to see how you can modify the plan as the action takes place, and how you can turn into a positive what other judoka are perceiving as a negative.

A number of years ago I was scheduled to participate in a competition, but because of organizational problems, the program ran very, very late. It was clear that we would still be fighting far into the night. I resigned myself to that fact, did my relaxation exercises, and tried to enjoy my waiting time as much as possible. As I talked to other competitors, I found myself hoping that the tournament would run even later because the longer the tournament ran, the more energy my opponents wasted by getting upset and complaining about matters over which they had no control!

PERFECTING THE MATCH PLAN

The match plan is not only about your opponent. In fact, it is mostly about finding a way to compete at your best in varying situations. The World Masters Judo Federation held the 2003 World Masters Championships at the Kodokan in Japan. Everyone believed it would be the biggest and toughest masters judo event to date, and indeed I believed it was. With all the different ages and weights as well as different categories for kata, there were close to a thousand master judo competitors.

Unfortunately, I had a severe injury to my right hip, painful to the point that a year later I would have to have the hip replaced. If I walked diagonally in the wrong direction, I would often simply fall down. Fortunately, I could move in other directions with relatively little discomfort.

As part of my match plan, I decided that with the correct strategy I could work around the injury. This strategy was to fight left-handed only so most of my pivoting was done on my left leg. I would use mostly a one-handed grip. If I had to fight two-handed, I would use a double lapel grip, allowing me to attack right and left.

Next I limited my throws to those that were really difficult to counter and were least affected by my hip injury. I chose four throws: leg picks, drop right seoi nage, left kouchigari, and left tomoe nage. I knew also that by using blocks and stumbles, I could still attack to all four corners of my opponent's stance.

The World Masters Championships is usually a five-day competition, and I was competing on the fourth day. For the first two days, I studied the refereeing. Most of the officials were from Japan, and almost all the referees, even those from Europe, were very lenient on false attack penalties (see chapter 1, article 19). Furthermore, from past experience I knew that referees do not enforce noncombative rules as strictly as the referees in the senior competitions do. These referees would allow players a little more time to set up their throws.

Armed with this information, I laid out a general tactical plan. Because master competition matches are only 3 minutes long, coming back from behind is very difficult. I knew I would have to come out very hard and fast. In my case, this meant fighting from a one-handed grip while fanning my arm. This procedure accomplished two goals: First, it helped me set up for throws; and second, it made it difficult for my opponent to attack. I would take any attacking opportunity that used the techniques I could perform with a one-handed grip. My defense on the ground (newaza) was sound, so I decided I could risk attacking with my throw full out and then follow up with a ground move if necessary. I know that the first one to secure a grip and apply a strong attack has the first chance to score, and the first one to score is in charge of the match. Once you get the first score, uke has to come after you. This pressure to catch up puts uke into a vulnerable situation.

In a 3-minute fight, you have approximately six scrimmages. Each scrimmage generally lasts 25 to 45 seconds. Win each of those and you have won the match.

PLANNING FOR SPECIFIC OPPONENTS

When considering the opponents I will be fighting, I first eliminate all judoka from the other pool. I have no idea who might come through to meet me in the final, so I eliminate worrying about that problem!

This is the same philosophy I have for the other quarter of my draw. I must look at my quota of the draw in a general, analytical way, sticking to basic generalizations: tall, short, right, left. My main focus is always on my immediate fight—first general and then specific—focusing on my opponent's arousal level when he is at the side of the mat.

Fight 1

In my first match, I had the advantage of knowing my opponent because he was a teammate of mine when I was on the British team. I knew he was a very skillful thrower with a low center of balance but not very physically intimidating, a quality he used to great advantage. He would often come out as very soft and gentle, luring his opponent to a false sense of security and then, Wham! he would slip under his opponent's center of balance with some form of hip throw. Knowing this, my match plan was to follow the general plan I had created, but first to be wary of getting lured in by his slow, gentle style. I knew I had to grip one-handed as much as possible because my opponent would need two hands on me to use his hip throws. As a result, after a hard fight, I managed to throw him for a koka with a leg pick and then held him down with yokoshiho gatame for ippon.

Fight 2

My second fight was against a Ukrainian fighter. My general impressions were that he had handily beat a good Russian fighter in his first round by throws and counters but attempted no groundwork at all. Nevertheless, it was obvious that he knew what he was doing in standing techniques. Physically we were similar in stature, but he was a lefty. My match plan was to stick to a general plan of applying a lot of stumbles and also takedowns into newaza, keeping active so as to either get a score or inflict a penalty. The outcome was a win for me by negating his judo, thus stalling him out until he received hansoku-maka.

Fight 3

In my third fight, I went up against a Yugoslavian fighter. My general impression was that he was tall and lean and looked very strong. He handled all of his opponents easily by securing a powerful over-the-back grip and rolling each over in some makikomi fashion to take them to the ground and finish them off.

My match plan, my general plan, had to be adapted. I decided that I must grip to the right first to control his right sleeve. When he tried to free his sleeve, I had to attack to the right side. At no time could I settle for an equal gripping situation. I was very happy to win by a wazari (half point) from a drop ippon seoi nage.

Fight 4

For the final, I was up against a Japanese fighter. I was in the first semifinal and thus had the luxury of watching the second semifinal that would decide who I would meet in the final. It was fortunate as well that my teammates had been scouting that side of the pool for me.

My general impressions of this fighter were that he was tall and skillful, seemed a little overconfident, displayed good tachi waza and newaza, used a right-handed collar grip, and executed rhythmical movements to set up his opponent with a minimum of two or three steps to enter any throws. When there was a flurry of action, he would ride it out and then regain control over his opponent.

My specific tactics were to disrupt his flow of movement by using a lot of one-handed fighting and blocks and stumbles. Because this is a tiring strategy, when I was in control on the ground I would eat up as much time as possible so as to recover.

As we were bowing in, he did not look at me. Instead he looked into the stands and nodded, a clear sign that his mind was not fully focused on me but on how he would look in front of his friends. I seized on this momentary lapse of concentration and went in for an attack as soon as possible. I took hold and threw him for a koka (quarter point), which put me in charge of the pace of the match. I was happy to win by the scores of koka and then an ippon with drop seoi nage.

I had designed a match plan and then successive specific plans based on prior knowledge and prematch scouting. I modified my plans as necessary. Preparation paid off.

PART III

Competition

9

Building Aerobic and Anaerobic Endurance

By using time analysis of judo matches, we can identify the roles of both the aerobic and anaerobic systems in judo. Analyzing the energy requirements for judo, however, is a little more challenging because judo competitors use all energy systems during training and competitions. The fact that judo is a sport with stop time makes it even more difficult to analyze. When there is a break in the action, the officials stop the fight and bring the judoka back to the middle of the mat to restart the fight. Depending on the circumstances, this rest phase may take 10 to 40 seconds. If a combatant's gi needs to be tied, for example, the rest phase may be up to 40 seconds. The work phase, or action of the match, may last as little as 5 seconds or as long as 60 seconds. Seldom does a work phase last longer than 60 seconds. The mean time for a work phase is 30 seconds.

The duration and intensity of the work and rest periods vary dramatically, but seldom during a hard 5-minute fight is a rest interval long enough to deal fully with the high demands of recovery from repeated use of the anaerobic lactic system. This debt is worse if the athlete goes into golden score. As the fight goes on, the judoka must tolerate ever-increasing amounts of lactic acid. The situation is complicated by the fact that at major events a judoka may have five or six matches in one day. Often there is insufficient time to recover fully from previous fights. Taking all of these factors into consideration, one can see that a judoka must train all energy systems to the limit.

AEROBIC ENERGY SYSTEM

The term *aerobic* refers to the use of oxygen. The intensity of aerobic exercise is low enough that the heart and lungs are able to supply oxygen to the working muscles. The aerobic energy system kicks in 2 to 3 minutes after activity begins and lasts for about 12 minutes of continuous movement. Aerobic exercise uses the major muscle groups, including the legs and buttocks, and is done at an intensity that gets you breathing deeply but not so hard that you are out of breath. A more formal description of aerobic exercise is an activity that requires from 60 to 80 percent of your maximum heart rate, depending on your fitness level.

Swimming, biking, rowing, and running are common aerobic exercises. Running is believed to have the most beneficial crossover effect for judo, but the others are certainly good alternatives if you cannot run because of injury or weather conditions. You can improve aerobic fitness by using other energy systems, but because of the intensity of these activities (e.g., interval training), they are not considered classical aerobic exercise.

A well-developed aerobic system benefits a judoka in three ways. First, it improves $\dot{V}O_2$max, which is an indicator of how much oxygen the body can hold and use during exercise. Any improvement in the body's ability to use oxygen is limited by genetics, but training can improve your potential for using oxygen by 10 to 20 percent. A high $\dot{V}O_2$max is desirable because it indicates a greater potential for fitness. However, an untrained judo athlete who has a higher $\dot{V}O_2$max will not enjoy the other aerobic benefits that an aerobically trained athlete with a lower $\dot{V}O_2$max will enjoy.

A second benefit of proper aerobic training is that it raises your aerobic threshold. This allows you to work at a higher intensity before moving from an aerobic to an anaerobic system. This delays the onset of fatigue from lactic acid production and allows a higher volume of training.

The third benefit is the clearance of lactic acid. During all highly contested judo matches, an extremely high amount of lactic acid is produced. A judoka who has a well-developed aerobic system can clear this buildup of lactic acid from the muscles, reducing fatigue and muscle soreness.

Think of the implications of these three benefits. Developing your aerobic energy system increases your potential to improve all aspects of fitness. You will be able to train longer and harder because you will recover from practices and matches more efficiently. You will be able to train and fight at a higher intensity before needing your anaerobic system, which has its limitations. You will produce less lactic acid during a fight and be more efficient at clearing lactic acid from the muscles during the rest phases of a match (matte) as well as between matches. For your second, third, and fourth matches, you will start with less lactic acid residue in your body than your aerobically unfit opponent. With less lactic acid in your muscles during the final minutes of a fight, you will be able to maintain a high level of intensity as your less fit opponent lowers his intensity because his lactic acid levels are increasing.

Aerobic fitness has a systemic effect on the body, benefiting every bodily function. This spins off into many health benefits, making an active lifestyle more realistic and more enjoyable. The better your overall health, the better judoka you will become.

ANAEROBIC ENERGY SYSTEM

Anaerobic refers to the absence of oxygen. When you are working in the anaerobic system, you do not have to rely on fresh oxygen from the heart and lungs to assist in the fueling process for the muscles that are in use. This is the opposite of what happens when the body is using the aerobic system. The anaerobic system uses the fuel and oxygen already stored in the muscle. This stored energy allows you to train at a very high intensity for a relatively short period of time. When the stored fuel runs out, you have to lower the intensity of the activity and rely on the aerobic system or stop the activity altogether.

The anaerobic system has two categories: the anaerobic alactic system and the anaerobic lactic system. The anaerobic alactic system does not produce lactic acid. This system can be used for extremely high-intensity activities that last no more than 5 seconds. Maximum effort (95 to 100 percent intensity) can be used with this system because there is no need for any conversion of fuel sources to feed the working muscle. When training the alactic system, improvements come from neuromuscular patterning and increased strength gains more than from the adaptation of muscle fibers or the conversion or tolerance of any fuel sources or their by-products such as lactic acid. Any simple explosive throwing movement or explosive lifting movement helps develop the anaerobic alactic system. You use the anaerobic alactic system every time you apply maximum force during judo—for example, when you throw, when you make your initial bridging action, when you escape from a pin, or when you break off an opponent's grip.

The anaerobic lactic system produces lactic acid. This system starts where the anaerobic alactic system leaves off and can be maintained for approximetely 2 minutes, depending on the athlete's conditioning. The intensity of training in this system ranges from approximately 75 to 95 percent of maximum heart rate. I say *approximately* because with appropriate drills this is the most trainable of all the energy systems. In addition, the anaerobic lactic system can be trained with the same exercises used in aerobic training or anaerobic alactic training; simply change the intensity, speed, and duration of the exercises while varying the rest periods to pull in the anaerobic lactic system.

The anaerobic lactic system comes into play during the gripping and grappling actions of a fight, as you try to set up uke for a throw, or as you transition from standing to groundwork. You can use this energy system for any activities that last longer than 5 seconds but less than 2 minutes. With a well-developed anaerobic lactic system, you can string longer chains of continuous judo skills or apply more skills more frequently.

COMBINATION OF ENERGY SYSTEMS

Many people mistakenly believe that at any given time a person is using only one of the energy systems. This is not so; even when you are squarely in the middle of the anaerobic lactic system, for example, you are receiving help from the anaerobic alactic and aerobic systems. All three systems work hard to assist each other, depending on the intensity of the activity. One system may have a more dominant roll in the assisting process, but at all times all three systems are involved to some degree. Table 9.1 illustrates this point.

Table 9.1   Percentage of Energy Systems Involved When Maximum Available Force Is Applied

Time	Aerobic	Anaerobic alactic	Anaerobic lactic
10 seconds	15%	50%	35%
30 seconds	20%	15%	65%
2 minutes	50%	4%	46%
10 minutes	90%	1%	9%

Judo Canada NCCP Proposed Coaching Manual.

JUDO DRILLS TO DEVELOP THE AEROBIC ENERGY SYSTEM

To design drills for any energy system, you must look at the parameters needed to improve that energy system—intensity, duration, and frequency. The two ways to develop the aerobic system are through traditional aerobic exercises and through interval training.

Traditional aerobic exercises use the long, slow duration (LSD) method. These exercises should be the cornerstone of aerobic training. They should be performed throughout the year for the systemic health benefits as well as the judo benefits. The intensity of the LSD method is 60 to 80 percent maximum heart rate. The duration for a judoka should be 20 to 45 minutes, and the frequency should be two to four times a week. Obviously, the lower the intensity is, the longer the duration should be. The frequency must change to correspond with the training season.

The aerobic system can also be developed using interval training. This can be achieved in a number of ways, but when designing your drills and training program, focus on intensity (80 to 95 percent of maximum heart rate), duration (3 to 5 minutes, five sets or bouts, with 5-minute rest periods between bouts), and frequency (twice a week, depending on the training season). Again, remember that the higher the intensity is, the shorter the duration should be.

Try randori drills in newaza, tachi waza, or a combination of the two. Randori drills require judoka of approximately equal ability. Each must have a sound understanding of the requirement of the drill, which is to fight aggressively with energetic (intense) movement and frequent attacks. This drill is often more effective when a third party acts as an official and keeps the movement flowing (figure 9.1).

Figure 9.1 Judoka practicing randori.

When you have an imbalance of skill or power, it is often more beneficial for the strongest judoka to face a lineup of weaker opponents. This might mean selecting five weaker judoka to fight the stronger judoka for 1 minute each. This particular drill is a challenging aerobic training tool only if there is not a large discrepancy among the ability or fitness of the judoka. To lessen the duration, simply remove judoka from the lineup. Another way to modify this drill would be to lessen the intensity and maintain the duration. Or you could reduce the number of opponents but increase each opponent's time fighting the stronger judoka. Again, a third party should act as an official to keep the action moving.

Gripping drills also can work using a lineup format. Try to control your opponent by outgripping him. Your aim is to put uke into a defensive position or drag him to his knees to win (figure 9.2). The interaction can be very intense as both you and your opponent try to get your preferred grip or as each rips off the other's grip. Again, to add intensity, simply shorten uke's workout against you.

An often overlooked element of these drills is that uke benefits by learning how to be very intense for a short period of time. These drills develop the aggressive attitude needed in higher-level competition.

Figure 9.2   Gripping drill.

JUDO DRILLS TO DEVELOP ANAEROBIC ENERGY

As with the aerobic system, you must respect the training parameters of the chosen energy system before designing a drill to train the anaerobic energy systems. For such drills, go for an intensity of 90 to 100 percent maximum heart rate, a duration of 30 to 120 seconds for each drill, a rest phase two to three times greater than the work interval, and a frequency of twice a week. Supplement skill-specific anaerobic training with generic anaerobic training twice a week. The goal of these drills is to develop the ability to maintain maximum intensity for longer periods of time. Note: Skill or intensity must never suffer in order to finish a drill. As soon as the skill level of the activity or the intensity of the activity deteriorates, the drill must stop.

Before you do any anaerobic work, warm up completely. Include some light aerobic exercises and stretches. Be sure you are not fatigued; anaerobic training must be done while you are fresh.

Uchikomi

Uchikomi is so versatile that there are no limits to the manipulations of its forms in developing fitness. Following is a list of suggestions for uchikomi drills. Seldom can skill and intensity be maintained for the higher limits of the anaerobic system. Uchikomi is preferable for shorter durations.

• **Basic uchikomi**. Perform speed uchikomi on uke, coming full in and out on uke (figure 9.3). Start with your feet square each time. If your skill deteriorates, the drill is over. Always drill in good form.

• **Alternating uchikomi**. Attack uke, then fully step out and stand square to uke. Uke then attacks you. Take turns attacking. Use uke's rotating out as part of your pull as you go into your throw. The movement must be realistic; both you and uke should fully come in and out. This action of coming fully in and out should take up at least the length of one tatami mat space. This is a good tool for practicing all entries: front, back, and on both sides.

Figure 9.3   Basic uchikomi.

• **Circling uchikomi**. Attack uke with taiotoshi. Uke steps over your leg and completes the circle by facing you square on. At this point, step to the head of the triangle made by your foot and uke's two feet and follow up with osotogari. Uke then steps off the osotogari and pushes back toward you. Using the momentum created, apply another taiotoshi. Repeat the sequence until the time has elapsed.

• **Throwing drills**. For throwing lines, you will need three or four willing partners (figure 9.4). Throw each partner for an appropriate amount of time; then rest and repeat. For the safety of uke and the development of skill, if your technique or control deteriorates, stop the drill. A crash mat may be used to make this drill easier on uke.

Another good throwing drill is the throw-and-pick-up-drill. This drill is very demanding, but I find it useful. For version 1, throw uke but keep hold of uke with both hands after he falls. As uke starts to get up, start to pull for your next throw. Throw uke again. Repeat until the time has elapsed.

In version 2 of the throw-and-pick-up-drill, you do the drill while making a circle around the outside of the whole tatami. Throw uke but maintain a hold only on uke's sleeve. After uke falls, run in a half circle in front of uke and wait for him to get up. As uke rises, regrab his sleeve and throw him again. In this version, you pull less but allow the combination of uke's rising from the ground and your subtle pull to develop your conditioning and timing.

Figure 9.4   Throwing lines drill.

Randori

Randori drills are much better suited for the longer durations needed to develop the anaerobic energy systems.

- **Two-on-one newaza**. In this drill, two judoka work to pin uke (figure 9.5). No one uses chokes or armlocks. The two judoka must work in unison

Figure 9.5   Two-on-one newaza.

to avoid injuries by both pulling uke in different directions. This is a fun and exhausting drill. A variation on this drill requires two judoka to hold uke down. To make the escape more realistic, handicap the two judoka so they can use only one hand each. If uke is much stronger, simply do not handicap the two judoka who are holding him down.

• **Randori in either newaza or tachi waza**. If you have a strong training partner of equal strength and fitness to yourself, use each other's strength. Perform a very hard shift of randori for an appropriate length of time; then rest for the required time. Repeat until the drill is completed. Use a third party to act as an official to keep the intensity level high.

• **Lineups**. This is basically the same drill as described in the section on aerobic drills but from a different perspective. This time, perform the single 1-minute or 2-minute drill all out. Rest 2 to 4 minutes, and then repeat. If you are much stronger than uke, get two or three opponents to do 30-second to 40-second shifts to add intensity.

By no means does this list exhaust the number of drills to develop the anaerobic energy systems, but it gives you a good idea as to how to design your own drills. That is the key element.

JUDO DRILLS TO DEVELOP THE ANAEROBIC ALACTIC SYSTEM

The development of the anaerobic alactic system comes mostly through strength training and explosive lifting or throwing movements. A few judo drills are useful, mostly throwing drills. They are more effective if you finish the throw by following the opponent down and then rolling across and over uke's body.

All drills are done in sets of five with 10- to 15-second rests between throws and 5-minute rests between sets. Perform three or four sets per workout twice a week.

• **Throwing drill 1**. Attack with an appropriate grip. Walk around the mat with uke and apply an explosive throw. Follow uke to the mat and roll across and over uke's body.

• **Throwing drill 2**. You need two opponents and a crash mat for this drill. Take hold of uke in a normal fashion. As a teammate holds uke by the collar and belt, attack uke with a throw while putting out as much effort as you can. Your teammate holds back uke from being thrown for 1 to 2 seconds. Your teammate then lets go of uke, allowing you to complete the throw. Your teammate must not push or pull uke or he will throw tori off his proper form. Also, you must not break form to try to get more power or leverage.

TACTICS AND CONDITIONING

Specific judo drills can be combined with tactical training and match preparation to develop specific energy systems. These drills can be practiced with one or more partners.

The drills already covered in this chapter have focused on conditioning because skill development is common in judo through uchikomi and nagekomi and such. Tactics seem to be left to chance, either to randori or to hard-gained match experience in actual tournaments. The drills covered here are not new. Many of these drills were common to British national team members in the 1960s and 1970s. My experience traveling and training in other countries showed me that they are widespread.

Many judoka consider drills as a way to fill time rather than a legitimate training tool, as just something to warm you up for randori. This attitude is a huge mistake. A properly designed drill can have all the elements of randori with a much more specific focus and more intensity than traditional randori. And drills are vital to understanding and applying tactics.

In this book, I have described grips, entries, and throws as well as takedowns and ground techniques. These techniques were not included so you could use all of them as offensive tools. The descriptions are meant to make you familiar with techniques and help you handle very specific situations when they arise. The descriptions present concepts on which to base tactics.

The most effective way to develop tactics is to drill them. Consider your experience in both offensive and defensive situations. It may be that when you get a grip in a particular attack situation, you realize you have a limitation. So you decide to expand the variety of throws you can use from that grip. Maybe you want to drill a counter throw in a defensive situation, or develop a technique to enable you to escape from a particular throw or grip with which you are having trouble. Once you know what you want, line up five or six teammates and ask them to grip in a particular way so that you can react properly. Use that drill until the movement becomes second nature.

All situations can be improved by drilling combined elements of judo and entering thoughtfully through the gates of gripping, circling, entering, throwing, using takedowns, and transitioning into specific ground skills. Any of these can be used either as offensive or defensive tools.

A judoka's time and energy are at a premium. The more efficient you can be with drill design, the better. Here are some thoughts to help you design tactical drills.

When learning new skills or tactics, never sacrifice proper form for speed or conditioning. Once you have mastered the drill, find as many uses for it as possible. Use it to condition your body while adding new throws from the now familiar grip and circling pattern mat awareness.

Drills can be made up of parts of the whole chain of events; sequences of two or three parts; or the linking together of individual skills by parts, sequences of two or three skills, or the whole chain (gripping, circling, throwing, and transitioning to ground skills).

Only when skills are automatic do you add intensity. As soon as you feel comfortable with the added intensity, start to use the drills as conditioning tools.

Unfamiliar Grips

Often judoka from a small dojo have limited randori patterns and few, if any, left-handed partners. As a result, they may feel uncertain against a left-handed opponent. To fix this problem, tori should ask four teammates to line up and come at him one at a time, each gripping left-handed. Tori gets his grip, circles in the appropriate direction, and throws uke. Tori follows the process with each teammate. Tori gradually increases the speed of the drill until a traditional left-handed grip feels comfortable at full intensity; this may take several weeks. Tori, who was previously comfortable only with a traditional grip, can start asking for over-the-back left-handed grips or sleeve back grips to the left side. At this point, tori may want to practice ripping off a left-handed grip and then completing a throw. There are many options.

Mat Awareness

A common judo tactic is to force the opponent out of bounds or make the opponent stand in the safety area for more than 5 seconds, hoping that the opponent receives a penalty. A progression of self-designed drills for this situation is possible. For example, start with your back to the red mat. Have your opponent try to push you out. Act accordingly to avoid stepping out of the area. Reverse positions and continue the process.

This method allows you to study both sides of the situation. You could then repeat the drill and ask uke to respond with the most common reaction. Apply a throw using uke's movement as he reacts. Finally, repeat the process with both of you having the freedom to move as you see fit, either to throw or simply evade the situation. If you want to add a conditioning element, have two or three teammates take turns until your work phase is completed.

Controlling Time in the Match

A number of situations may arise in a match in which you must control the pace or openness of the fight. Your actions will vary depending on whether you're winning or losing (keep in mind that losing by a penalty is a different situation than losing by a score). You must study all of these situations and design drills for each. Being able to design drills for your own needs is crucial.

For example, imagine a situation in which you are winning by koka with 1 minute left in the match. If you make a tactical error, you could be penalized.

This could tie the match, or you could lose it. This is when understanding the intent of the rule is as important as understanding the letter of the rule. Let's say you just scored with 1 minute left. In the next flurry of action, you drop your head, straighten your arms, and slightly retract your hips. Right now you are at great risk of immediately receiving a penalty for passivity. If you did the same thing in a tied match or if you were losing, the referee would not be so acutely concerned with your defensive intent. You need to drill to get through that last minute without being scored on or penalized.

Even though you're tired, your body position is key. Remember, keep your head and hands up and circle. Now might be a great time to use a one-handed grip. Fan your arm to stop uke from getting a strong grip. If you're confident on the ground, a safe kata guruma attack may be appropriate. If not, you might use a block or a stumble to meet the requirement to attack every 15 seconds, and then jump on uke's back to eat up another 15 seconds by looking busy.

That's half the time gone. Now it's vital for your body language to say, Come on! Let's fight! while your gripping strategy indicates to uke that there is no way you are getting into a good scoring position. Such match awareness comes from years of hard-learned lessons while winning, and often losing, close-fought matches. The training time for this skill can be drastically reduced by drilling judo skills for conditioning and tactics.

Have someone act as an official when you drill in this manner. The presence of an official affects your awareness of rules and your tactical sense as you drill.

The situations and tactical combinations are endless. What is important is that you learn to identify weak spots in your own judo and that you and your teammates work together to design drills. Use the guidelines presented in this chapter to strengthen weak links in your armor. In high-level competition, it is not always the judoka with the best throw or hold who wins. More often the winner is the most consistent judoka who has a solid all-around tactical plan.

10

Increasing Judo-Specific Strength and Speed

Judoka use different types of speed and strength throughout a judo contest—absolute speed, reactive speed, maximum strength, power, and isometric strength. It would take an entire book to cover such a complex topic fully, but I will cover some basics and some time-proven drills to increase speed and strength for judo.

SPEED-SPECIFIC TRAINING

A number of factors affect speed, including maximum strength, muscle coordination (can your hamstring fully relax when your thigh contracts so as to work efficiently as one unit?), and the amount of fast-twitch muscle fiber you recruit when you forcefully contract the muscle. A factor I call *perceived quickness*, or speed, is in direct relation to how efficiently you position your body before you attack to lessen your body's need for movement in applying the attack. Skill and technique efficiency also affect speed.

In chapter 3 in the sidebar titled "The Sound of Uchikomi," I described how the efficient uchikomi foot pattern is *soft*, heavy, heavy, with the soft step to the head of the triangle made from uke's two feet and your leading foot. If that step were so subtle as to seem insignificant to uke, you would have accomplished two important goals: You would have saved your power for the finish (the two heavy steps), and uke would have less warning of the attack and less time to react to it and thus, your attack would be perceived as being faster than it really was.

The order in which you move your limbs or the sequence of the kinetic chain while rotating into a forward throw is crucial. Often when a judoka attacks, his hips, shoulders, and head move as if they were one unit. To create real speed, however, the judoka must lead with the hips and then the shoulders. Only when the shoulders are almost fully rotated does the head whip around, providing the impetus for a strong finish to the throw.

Hand Speed

As you learned in the discussion of gripping in chapter 2, hand speed is very important for cross gripping and gaining the first grip. The ability to jab your arm out and snatch your opponent's gi is invaluable when fighting for a grip.

In these drills, you rehearse the skills of maneuvering into throwing position and getting through uke's defenses and simultaneously develop hand and foot speed.

The first drill is borrowed from boxing. Begin shadowboxing by moving around the mat alone as you would in randori. Throw punches out as quickly and in as relaxed a manner as possible.

The second drill is identical in principle to shadowboxing. In shadow uchikomi, visualize yourself having a gripping fight. It is very important to visualize the smallest details possible and to move exactly as you would in the real situation. As the movements become more natural, increase the rapidity of your movements until you are at top speed. In phase 2 of this drill, obtain the imagined grip and follow it up with an imagined throw.

The third drill is a game drill between you and a partner. The goal of the game is to flick your opponent down to his knees by using various gripping tactics. The objective of the game is to use appropriate circling principles while recognizing and exploring weaknesses in uke's body position. I use this game in speed development because gripping and circling movements must be performed in a smooth, rapid action with a flicking movement at the end to unbalance uke. In the game, tori may use a blocking movement but may not attempt a throw to get uke to the ground.

The fourth drill is another game designed to develop a tactical sense of how to maneuver yourself into scoring position. The object of the game is for either you or your opponent to pick up the other. The game ends when either player earns five points. A player gains one point by picking up one of his opponent's feet from the mat while still retaining one hand on uke's gi. A player gets two points by getting through uke's defenses and picking up both of uke's feet while gripping in a front-on bear hug position. Finally, a player can get three points for getting behind uke and lifting uke up off both his feet.

Rotational Speed

The manner and effectiveness of body movement has a big influence on the speed of the movement. To create speed in your attack, you must position your body in the correct position in relation to uke's body, relax the muscles that are not in use, and understand the order in which specific joints come into play throughout the rotation.

The first drill is a solo stepping-in entry (see page 89). The stepping-in entry (right-sided) develops speed in the rotational action of a forward throw. Perform this drill solo. Stand at the end of a mat. Bring your hands up as though you are holding uke's gi in a lapel collar grip. Casually step forward with your right foot, slightly to the left of the center of the mat. Think of the outside edge of the mat as uke's shoulders and imagine uke's squared-up feet as being slightly narrower than the shoulders. Maintain a bend in your right leg as you bring your left foot back in a semicircle. Be careful not to go past your right foot or it will cause a momentary weakness for you in the backward direction. Stamp your left foot as it makes contact with the mat and use the impetus of the stomp, in conjunction with the straightening of the right leg, to bring your body up and rotate to the right. Drive your right lapel hand straight up, envisioning that you pull uke onto his toes as you straighten your right leg. At the end of the rotation, step your right foot across and down forcefully. Square up and repeat the drill, facing in the opposite direction.

The order of the joints involved in assisting the rotation is hip, shoulders, and then head. This solo entry is excellent as a study tool or a warm-up and is effective for throws such as taiotoshi, seoi nage, ouchigari, and taniotoshi because all of these throws can be performed from this one position.

The second drill is a solo stepping-away entry (see page 88). For this drill, stand at the end of a mat and visualize all of the movements as in the first drill. Now take a step back with your right foot. If you point your right heel a little past 90 degrees, this assists in the rotation process. Take a step back with your left foot to the extent that your left foot is nearly facing forward. The left foot should land forcefully. Finish the rotation by bringing the right foot parallel to the left. The right foot must also land with force. The order of joint progression is the same as for the stepping-in entry: hip, shoulder, and then head.

Do not underestimate the value of these drills in developing speed of entry and basic throwing patterns.

Speed Drills With Resistance

Solo uchikomi with rubber tubing is a great way to add resistance to your drill without hindering either your movements or the form of the rotational movement (figure 10.1). When concentrating purely on speed and agility, you can use a lighter weight of rubber cord. When you are working on power and commitment, use a heavier resistance such as bicycle tubing tied together. Either piece of tubing must be long enough so that you can keep both hands in front of your shoulders throughout the full rotation. Check the tubing for tears before each use because they do wear out.

For speed, start by wrapping the rubber tubing around a secure post. Face the post. You can perform either a stepping-in or stepping-away entry, but note that stepping-away entries require a slightly longer piece of tubing. For

Figure 10.1   Solo uchikomi with a rubber tube.

speed or drop entries, keep your body erect and do your entry exactly as you would a solo entry. When coming out of the entry, pull your right hand back at about shoulder height until you feel tension; then allow the recoil to assist you in your next entry. This really helps your timing and rhythm and adds a little more speed.

When you are trying to generate more power, the throw has a different feel to it. You can add much more commitment to the movement because the inner tubes will carry your weight. For power, fully rotate to the point of no return for your imagery uke. This drill is a great tool for developing both speed and power.

Accelerated Uchikomi

Accelerated uchikomi is a process by which you start uchikomi very slowly and then progressively increase the speed over the next five or six uchikomi until you are at top speed. Once you hit top speed, throw! Note: You must start very slowly if you wish to hit top speed.

Reactive Speed

Reactive speed training increases the speed with which you react to an action. This is the same as reaction time, the time it takes to recognize an attack or counter. The action can be either solely from uke or a reaction you encouraged from uke.

The blind uchikomi drill develops a feel or instinct for the proper moment in which to take advantage of uke's vulnerable situation. Uke and yourself both take an opposite sleeve lapel grip (a double lapel grip also works). In this situation, some judoka prefer their lapel grip to be under their opponent's arm, whereas some prefer that it be over. When you are set, ask uke to change his lapel grip (see changing grip on page 92). As he does, go in for a throw.

What makes this such a useful drill is that your signal to attack is not that you see uke's hand movement but that you feel the freedom of your shoulder as uke releases his grip. At first it is easier to do this drill with your eyes closed, hence the name.

Once you are comfortable with the basic movements, add a tactical element. Move around the mat in randori fashion holding on to uke's lapel. Change your grip on the lapel either under or over uke's arm, but as you do, apply a close sasae block to uke's closest foot. This distraction, in addition to the element of surprise, should be enough to keep you safe from uke's putting in a strong attack as you change your grip. Uke, feeling uncomfortable with this change, will move to regain the original grip. The moment he lets go is the time for you to attack. This may sound a little overplanned, but it is a very effective and trainable drill. Once you are comfortable with this grip, move on to other gripping situations. Recognizing and capitalizing on moments of opportunity in transition moments of a fight will be beneficial throughout your competitive career.

Remember that speed training must be done at the beginning of a class when you are fresh. Repetitions should never last so long that you start to slow down after hitting peak speed. You should also try to incorporate your speed training with your anaerobic alactic training. As a rule, properly designed speed programs can be used throughout the year but are particularly emphasized during both the precompetition phase and the competition phase.

STRENGTH TRAINING FOR JUDO

In itself, judo is an excellent form of strength training. Just the act of pushing and pulling against the opponent's resistance produces a training response. In fact, some judoka claim that judo and wrestling are the best all-around strength-building activities for prepubescent children.

Strength training must be age appropriate. During and after puberty, strength-specific training using light weights and rubber tubing can be introduced. Loads of no more than 30 to 40 percent of a perceived maximum should be used during the first year. Limits of 50 to 65 percent may be used as the teenager grows into late puberty. The book *Total Training for Young Champions* by Tudor O. Bompa (2000, Human Kinetics) covers this topic very thoroughly.

Just as judo makes use of all three energy systems, so are its strength requirements extremely inclusive. Good strength is required in all three forms of muscle involvement: eccentric controlled downward movement (as in bending the legs to get into seoi nage), concentric movement (the straightening action as used in the drive upward to finish the seoi nage), and isometric movement (when the joints involved stay static, as in clamping in on a hold-down).

Judo requires different types of strong muscle contractions, as well as three different types of strength: maximum strength, strength endurance, and power. Maximum strength is the maximum force one can apply in a single movement against a given resistance. Developing maximum strength is vital. It protects against injuries and supplies a better base from which to develop both strength endurance and power. Maximum strength benefits are seen in kumi kata (grip fighting) and most newaza moves.

Strength endurance enables you to continuously apply a submaximal force over a given time period. The development of strength endurance improves the muscles' ability to resist fatigue in the presence of increasing amounts of lactic acid. Strength endurance's main benefit is allowing you to continue to perform at a high intensity in the presence of increasing amounts of lactic acid. From studying the energy systems and their recuperative time lines, we can see that it is impossible to fight a judo match at the needed intensity in a series of relatively long work and short rest phases (matte calls) and not produce lactic acid.

Power is the combination of speed and maximum strength. It is the ability to apply a great deal of force in one explosive movement. Power is used in all throwing actions and in escaping hold-downs.

Training Maximum Strength

A good weight program, developed from a number of sound routines, is the most effective way to improve maximum strength. Before recommending a program, I must caution that maximum strength training should be undertaken only by an athlete who has finished puberty and has a training background of a minimum of two years of weightlifting. If you have fewer than two years of weight training, you should train at lower intensities. This will produce a better foundation on which to build maximum strength with a reduced risk of injury. Even with light weights, a judoka who is new to this form of training can expect good strength gains.

A number of routines will develop maximum strength, but I prefer the maximum load method. It is effective and easy to follow. For more on this method, see *Periodization Training for Sports, Second Edition,* by Tudor O. Bompa and Michael Carrera (2005, Human Kinetics).

The maximum load program follows a light/medium/heavy cycle for the week, allowing you to share your limited energy with the other demanding aspects of judo training.

Maximum strength should be trained during the general preparation phase of your yearly program. This period also can include training in generic power movements. During the precompetition phase, pay increasing attention to power and less to maximum strength.

The Bompa program is 9 to 12 weeks long and goes in three-week cycles, with a test day at the end of each three-week group:

Load: 85 to 100 percent maximum

Number of exercises: 3 to 5

Number of repetitions: 1 to 4

Number of sets per session: 6 to 10

Rest intervals: 3 to 6 minutes between sets

Times for week: 2 or 3

I recommend that you keep to two times a week, particularly during the third week of each minicycle when the intensity will be high. The rationale is that judo is a hard sport for your body to recover from. With the added stress of heavy weights, you may have a difficult time recuperating fully.

Whatever exercise you choose to use, make sure you know how to perform each lift safely. When lifting these percentages of your maximum weight, you must be certain to use proper lifting technique.

Before starting the program, test your maximum single repetition, the maximum weight you can lift in one complete repetition. The repetition must be of good form without using momentum to assist the lift. Once you find your maximum single repetition, use that number to calculate the weight to use. If you can bench press 100 pounds once and no more, that would be your maximum single repetition. If the program called for 80 percent of your maximum single repetition, you would take 80 percent of 100 pounds to get 80 pounds, the weight you would use.

At the end of each three-week cycle, retest your maximum single repetition. Make sure you have at least one day (but preferably two days) of rest from your last weight workout before you retest. Your maximum single repetition should have gone up slightly; use your new results to find the new weights to use for your next three-week cycle.

Training Strength Endurance

Strength endurance can also be developed in a number of ways. This ability to handle large amounts of lactic acid and still perform is very beneficial to judo. The following program was introduced to me by André Sadjez, and it is the most effective weight program I have found for developing lactic acid tolerance.

Begin this program early in the precompetition phase of your yearly plan and follow it right up to the last week before a major competition. I have tried different variations of the program, and so far all have been effective. The most basic and easiest way to increase intensity is to add time to the work phase.

Perform the program in circuit fashion. Select five exercises, one each for legs, trunk, chest, and back, and then one all-out speed movement such as a stride jump. Perform the exercises at full speed with no rest between stations.

Start the program with 30 to 40 percent of the maximum single repetition of the exercise for a duration of 15 seconds. You should be doing slightly more than a repetition a second in most exercises. Go through the five exercises twice for a work time of 2.5 minutes, not including the time it takes to change stations. At the end of the circuit, immediately perform light aerobic exercise for 10 minutes. Repeat the circuit. Follow with 10 minutes of light aerobic exercise as a cool-down.

To add intensity, each week add 5 seconds to the duration of each exercise to a maximum of 30 seconds, creating a 5-minute work phase. Only highly trained and motivated judoka can push through this circuit for the 5 minutes. It is imperative that the speed of the exercise not drop for the sake of adding more time to the exercise. A partner who can time you and, more important, motivate you can be very beneficial. If you're not sure if you are working at the right intensity, there is an easy test: If you don't feel like throwing up at the end, you could have pushed more!

Training Power

Because power is a combination of maximum strength and speed, much of the information about training power has been included in those sections. Nevertheless, we need to address power separately. Introduce generic power exercises that focus on maximum power training during the general phase of training. Move to judo-specific power training during the precompetition phase of the yearly plan.

Modified Olympic lifting movements are effective in developing power. It isn't necessary to try to do full Olympic lifts. Olympic lifters train specifically for years to gain the flexibility and skill to perform these lifts. By isolating the benefit we are looking for from a lift such as a clean, we can reap the benefit for judo without specializing in Olympic lifting. Start the pulling action of the lift higher off the floor by using blocks or a power cage. The bar should be just above your knee. Eliminate the catch part of a clean and concentrate only on the pull. This lift is referred to as a modified high pull and has a positive effect throughout the entire body.

Perform three to five repetitions and three to six sets. Rest for 3 to 5 minutes between sets. Perform the lift twice a week and incorporate it into your maximum strength program. The lift will improve whole body power. The benefits will be seen particularly in pickups and blocking movements.

Judo-specific drills should also be used to develop power. Keep in mind that the more specific the drill, the better the transfer from maximum strength to usable power for judo. For example, by using heavy rubber tubing, you can perform power uchikomi to great effect. The tubing must be strong enough to hold your weight as you rotate fully with as much power and commitment as possible. Keep repetitions low, only three to five reps with extended rest periods between sets.

Three-person uchikomi (figure 10.2) is another judo-specific power drill. A teammate holds uke by the back of his belt and collar as tori drives in as forcefully as possible. Tori continues to drive, trying his utmost to throw uke for 2 or 3 seconds. Stop and repeat. Do no more than three reps, and then rotate positions during your rest phase.

In another variation, after driving for 2 or 3 seconds, your teammate lets go and allows you to complete the throw. Your form should not be distorted in the attempt to create more power. As you can imagine, this results in a heavy fall for uke and a crash mat should be used.

In ura nage pickups, uke wraps his arm around your neck and turns in as if to perform koshi guruma. Bend your knees, wrap your arms around uke's waist, and in as rapid a movement as possible lift uke up into the air in an ura nage fashion (figure 10.3). Uke should make himself as heavy as possible. Because the resistance is not particularly heavy, the action must be as fast as possible. Again, reps are low, three to five, and the rest period is long, maybe 10 times greater than the work phase.

Figure 10.2   Three-person uchikomi.

Figure 10.3   Ura nage pickups.

Although maximum strength and strength endurance are heavily used in judo, that does not mean that judo is the best way to develop these types of strength. You must use the most efficient types of training which would include using weights, rubber tubing, medicine balls, and explosive movements with body weight when designing a program. The next chapter goes into more detail about creating a judo-specific conditioning program. Four sample training programs are included to help you develop your own conditioning plan for success.

11

Creating a Judo Conditioning Program

When designing a training plan, follow these basic rules. First, keep it simple. Judoka and coaches often design elaborate programs that only an exercise physiologist could understand. All you need to know is the goal of each work-out, which energy system is to be developed, and how to monitor that system (for example, the talk test when training the aerobic system).

Second, build a foundation. Begin with generic exercises; then move to judo-specific exercises.

Third, design your program to combine as many benefits as possible. We all have limited time and limited energy. The more needs you can meet in one program or drill, the more efficiently you use your time and energy.

Fourth, start with minimums. Training is a little like Goldilocks' porridge—one may be too hot, another too cold, and another just right. The physical adaptation required to improve fitness cannot be forced. If the stimulus to adapt is too low, adaptation will not occur. If the stimulus is too high, over-training and possibly injury will result. Start at a lower intensity and build up. If you see measurable improvement, maintain that intensity as long as you continue to improve. Pushing longer or harder seldom dramatically improves results. If you are going to make a mistake in training, then slightly undertrain! An injury is painful and wastes time.

Finally, know and respect the goals of each training season. Trying to develop all aspects of fitness at once throughout the entire year not only would result in minimal improvement but also could lead to overtraining and burnout. The training year can be divided into four phases (off-season, general preparation, precompetition, and competition), each of which has a different priority.

During the preseason, which can last 8 to 10 weeks, your main focus is on building aerobic fitness. Divide the preseason in two phases. The first phase is the generic training phase. Use generic aerobic exercise such as running at 75 to 80 percent of maximum heart rate for 20 to 30 minutes, four times a week. During the second phase of the preseason, aerobic training is much more judo specific, incorporating randori and drills to produce the training effect. Perform bouts of 3 to 5 minutes of hard randori or drills a minimum of twice a week at an intensity that leaves you panting at the end of each bout. Supplement this training with running twice weekly because in the precompetition phase you need to introduce aerobic training using generic exercises such as running to produce the training effect.

The actual competitive season can be divided into three phases, each of which is two weeks long—an early phase, a late phase, and an unloading or tapering phase. The aerobic system is maintained throughout the competitive season with two 20-minute runs a week at an intensity of 75 to 80 percent maximum heart rate. (Note: The 20 minutes does not include a 5-minute warm-up and 10-minute cool-down.) Anaerobic training becomes much more judo specific during the competitive season as judoka incorporate a combination of judo drills into their training.

The off-season can last one to three months. The main fitness goals during the off-season are to maintain aerobic fitness by doing two or three moderate 20- to 30-minute runs a week and to increase maximum strength. Anaerobic alactic fitness is improved and maintained best by increasing strength. The off-season is also a great time to participate in aerobic sports such as soccer or swimming. In addition to maintaining aerobic fitness in the off-season, participating in recreational sports outside of judo can provide a mental boost through a change of scene and social interaction with other athletes.

MONITORING PERFORMANCE AND PROGRESS

I have often referred to the percentage of maximum heart rate, the maximum rate at which you can get your heart to beat. Usually this is measured in beats per minute. This measure is used as an indicator of the intensity at which you are training. From this you can determine which energy system you are primarily using.

When you exercise, your heart beats faster to meet the demand of supplying more blood, and thus more nutrients and oxygen, to the working muscles. As you work harder, the muscles demand more oxygen and the heart beats faster. When your heart can no longer keep up with the demand for oxygen, it reaches a point referred to as the aerobic threshold.

As aerobically fit athletes reach a heart rate of 75 to 80 percent maximum heart rate, they rely more heavily on the anaerobic system to continue to exercise. Remember, though, that all three systems work together to some degree. The heart keeps pumping faster, trying to feed even more oxygen to the active muscles. When your heart simply cannot pump any faster, you have reached your maximum heart rate.

Measure your heart rate with a heart monitor (a convenient device I often use with my athletes) or with your fingers. Place your index and middle finger on the artery that runs along the side of neck. Using a clock with a second hand, count the beat for 10 seconds and multiply by 6 to find the beats per minute.

If you want to find out your maximum heart rate, try the following test. (Note: This is a very challenging test and should be done only by fit individuals. You will have to push yourself to the limit of your fitness.)

Find a track and get a heart monitor, if possible. After a good warm-up, sprint down the straight part of the track and jog around the curve. Gradually build up the sprints from about 80 percent to 90 percent and then go all out, with two laps at each speed. This is known as running bends and straights. Monitor your heart rate every second rotation of the track. Do as many all-out sprints as you can until your heart rate no longer continues to rise.

This is not the most scientific way of finding maximum heart rate, but it works and it is accurate enough. This process suits the strength of most judoka because it is similar to the work and rest phase of a judo fight. If this is the first time you have been tested, you should try the test on two or three separate occasions until you are familiar with pushing yourself to this degree. Once you are confident that you have found your maximum heart rate, repeat the test once a year.

A formula can be used to assess fitness—220 minus your age equals your maximum heart rate—but this formula is relevant for only 70 percent of the population.

Once you know your maximum heart rate, it is simple to monitor the intensity of your uchikomi and judo drills. Take your heart rate at the end of each drill. You will quickly become familiar with the feeling of the different intensities and will develop an internal measuring device to gauge them.

TRAINING PLANS

A yearly training plan has four main phases: off-season, general preparation phase, precompetition phase, and competition phase. Each phase has specific goals that are considered prerequisites or foundations on which to build a successful competitive season. Remember, a fit, healthy, and happy person lays the foundation for being a great athlete!

Off-Season

Use the off-season to set yourself up for success for the whole training year. This phase can last one to three months. Rejuvenation is vitally important to a yearly training plan, and the off-season is when you concentrate most on

© Empics

Design your training plan with key competitions in mind. Make sure you are fit, healthy, and ready for the most important competitions on your calendar.

rejuvenation. As with other aspects of training, once you have built a foundation, you must maintain it throughout the year.

Rejuvenation is probably the most neglected aspect of training. Simply doing nothing is not an effective means of rejuvenation. In fact, it is probably one of the least effective means. As elite athletes know, as few as two weeks of inactivity causes detraining.

For an activity to be rejuvenating, it must be an activity of your own choosing, it must be challenging but not so much so that it produces negative stress effects, and you should feel better after the activity than you did before it. A rejuvenation activity can be physical (participating in a different sport such as rowing, biking, or hiking), mental (such as meditation or art or music lessons), or a combination of the two (such as yoga). In the off-season, you must rejuvenate not only physically but also mentally. The more inclusive you can be by combining your social, physiological, and mental needs, the better it will be for you.

During the off-season, review your long-term goals, acknowledging any successes and adjusting for any setbacks. Make a general plan for the next session, including the training camps and competitions you plan to attend.

Under the heading of goal setting, include finances. If you are one of the lucky few whose club, family, or country covers all your training and traveling expenses, you can simply skip this part. But if you are like the rest of us, your training expenses are paid through a combined effort of your family, your club, your country, and yourself. During the off-season, your time commitment to training is often lower so you may have time to raise funds for later in the year or at least take time to look into travel plans and financial obligations.

Fitness maintenance is vital during the off-season. You need to maintain the fitness and strength you worked hard for last season by doing the minimum required training. Aerobic training should be twice a week for 20 minutes at 70 to 80 percent maximum heart rate using any traditional aerobic exercise or judo randori. To maintain maximum strength, perform maximum strength training once a week. Pick three or four exercises, one of which should be a power move such as modified high pulls, and perform five sets of three to five repetitions at 80 to 90 percent of your maximum single repetition.

During the off-season, prepare your body for the demands of the general preparation phase. Rehabilitate injuries and balance out the strength of muscle groups to prevent injuries from occurring.

The three basic functions of a muscle are to act as a prime mover, moving the joint; to act as an antagonist or counterbalance, helping to control certain functions of the joint movement initiated by the prime mover; and to stabilize the other joint so the prime mover can apply more force to the chosen joint.

During the year, an imbalance between the flexors and extenders surrounding a joint can build up. This imbalance can extend to both sides of the body, as well as upper and lower. During the off-season, your main focus should be to correct these imbalances, develop the stabilizing function of the muscles, and strengthen the connective tissue. In *Periodization Training for Sports*, Bompa referred to this training as anatomical adaptation and provided the following guidelines.

The main goal for judo in this phase is to increase judo understanding and knowledge by using learning tools such as kata, teaching juniors, and practicing a self-defense aspect. The deeper you understand the principles of judo, the more easily you will learn new variations and moves to use in competition.

The off-season is the time to experiment with new moves, grips, and entries. Throughout the book, I have documented a number of grips, entries, throws, and ground moves that are popular in judo today; the off-season is the time to go through them, experiment, and to try to get a feel for them. Even if you never use these techniques as offensive tools, your deeper understanding of each move will serve you well as a base from which to design defensive strategies and tactics. For offensive tools, pick one new throw and one new ground move. Get an insight and a feel for those moves. Look at the rating system in chapter 3 when deciding whether to use a move. If the move is not listed, evaluate it in a similar fashion, on chance of scoring, ease of entry, risk of penalty, and risk of counter.

A typical 2-hour off-season practice may include the following:

15 minutes of general warm-up with light aerobics and belt stretching

10 minutes of tumbling and ukemi

5 minutes of shadow uchikomi

20 minutes of skill work (studying new moves)

15 minutes of agility training using judo moves

10 minutes of judo-specific games (pickup game, two-mat sumo, any program that gets your heart rate up and is fun and aggressive!)

20 to 30 minutes of tachi waza randori (keep it light and moving, trying new moves or variations of familiar ones)

20 to 30 minutes of newaza randori

5 to 10 minutes of cool-down

This session can be run with as few as two people, but four or more is recommended. Such a program should be used no more than twice a week.

A weekly off-season training schedule might include the following:

Day 1: Maximum strength training

Day 2: Judo lighter than day 4 (meets one day's aerobic requirement)

Day 3: Anatomical adaptation circuits

Day 4: Judo heavier than day 2 (meets one day's aerobic requirement)

Day 5: Anatomical adaptation circuits

Day 6: Active rest rejuvenation

Day 7: Active rest rejuvenation

This seven-day schedule can be manipulated in many ways. When designing your own schedule, keep the heavy judo day away from the maximum strength day. You could combine the anatomical adaptation circuit with an aerobic workout.

General Preparation Phase

The general preparation phase usually lasts 8 to 12 weeks. The main goals are to develop the aerobic energy system, increase maximum strength, and integrate new judo skills. To figure out when to start the general preparation, simply count backward on a calendar from the date of your major competition, remembering to allow two to six weeks for the competition phase, including tapering off.

The general preparation phase begins with general or nonspecific training and includes the integration of new skills learned during the off-season into your competitive judo repertoire. At this stage, you should have a sound understanding of the new skills and the entries to use with them that best suit your judo movement patterns. Introduce the new moves into your judo first by drilling, then in randori, then in low-pressure competition.

The general preparation begins by developing the aerobic system to recover more efficiently from bouts of high-intensity anaerobic intervals such as in matches or in training. At the beginning of the general preparation phase, the long, slow duration (LSD) method is preferred (see chapter 9). If you have followed your training program during the off-season, you should have maintained your aerobic fitness to a large degree, ensuring that this season you will start from a higher aerobic base than you did at the beginning of last season. If you maintain this year's increase in fitness, then next year you will start this phase with an even higher aerobic base. The LSD method requires 20 to 30 minutes of aerobic activity at 70 to 80 percent of maximum heart rate three or four times a week.

If you are practicing judo three or four times a week, it may be difficult to fit aerobic activity into your program. Aerobic activity, even just twice a week, has been proven to be beneficial. Try combining running with other activities and at a different time of the day throughout the week.

Weight training is the best form of training for maximum strength, and maximum strength training is best for developing anaerobic alactic conditioning. Maximum strength training has a major carryover effect on power.

During the general preparation phase, you must start to introduce basic linking skill drills to meet your judo goals. By combining small segments of skills, you can build a sequence for a throwing drill: First, concentrate on obtaining a specific grip, allowing uke to move in any reasonable direction that the grip will allow; then choose the appropriate throw for the situation. Be sure to use the correct circling pattern and entry for the throw. For example, consider the process of getting a sleeve collar grip:

1. Twist uke's shoulders by pulling on uke's sleeve and pushing uke's shoulder with your elbow.

2. As uke circles toward you to regain his strong stance, pull uke's sleeve up and out and enter with a stepping-away entry.

3. Pull uke onto your hip and apply uchimata.

For a transition drill, uke starts on his knees. Throw uke, concentrating on the hand action and body movement of the throw. Follow uke to the ground, following the most direct path into an appropriate ground move.

Once you can perform each individual drill smoothly, combine the throwing drill with the transition drill so that you start by throwing uke from a standing position and then follow up with a transition to groundwork followed by applying a ground move.

Once the drill becomes smooth and automatic, uke starts to add resistance. Hopefully during the off-season you added a new throw and ground move to your judo repertoire. The general preparation phase is the time to work on defense from different situations, and on different entries for your strongest throw from various situations through the use of stumbles and blocks as setups.

A 2-hour judo practice in the general preparation phase might include the following:

15 minutes of general warm-up with light aerobic and belt stretching

5 minutes of ukemi and tumbling

5 minutes of shadow uchikomi (this is not only a great warm-up, but it can introduce you to visualization skills)

20 minutes of timing and skill drills

20 to 30 minutes of tachi waza randori

15 minutes of newaza transition and skill drills

20 minutes of newaza randori

10 minutes of cool-down

The aerobic system is being developed during this practice, so randori must be performed continuously at a challenging but not exhausting intensity, or performed at a slightly higher intensity in 3- to 5-minute intervals with the 3-minute intervals being at the highest intensity. Practice judo three or four times a week during the general preparation phase. If you do four judo practices a week, do aerobic sessions only twice a week.

A weekly schedule for general preparation with judo practice a minimum of three days a week and training only once a day might look like this:

Day 1: Weights and running

Day 2: Judo

Day 3: Off

Day 4: Weights and running

Day 5: Judo

Day 6: Running

Day 7: Judo

A weekly schedule with judo practice four times a week, running twice a week, and weights twice a week might look like this:

Day 1: Weights

Day 2: Judo and running

Day 3: Judo

Day 4: Off

Day 5: Weights

Day 6: Judo and running

Day 7: Judo

As you can see, the volume of training in this phase is very high. In fact, it is the highest of all the phases. Often you must combine two training sessions on the same day. If possible, try to have 4 to 6 hours between sessions. If that is impossible, do your aerobic work after weights, 1 hour before judo, or immediately after judo.

A word of caution: You may feel a little tired during this phase of training because such a high volume of training is required. Therefore, it is recommended that you not compete during this phase.

Precompetition Phase

The precompetition phase can be thought of as part 2 of the general preparation phase. The main objective of this phase is to prepare you specifically for competition by developing the anaerobic system; by converting maximum strength into power and speed endurance (increasing lactic acid tolerance); and by introducing simulation training and tactical awareness into your judo by way of drills, pressure training, and mock (or lower-pressure) match competitions. Because it is very intense, this phase is relatively short—four to six weeks. Even well-trained judoka cannot maintain such an intensity for very long.

© Empics

The precompetition phase is the most physically demanding, but it will prepare you for competition by improving anaerobic fitness, increasing your stamina, and developing tactical awareness.

As the intensity of training increases, the volume of training goes down and the need for recovery increases. In the precompetition phase, the more efficient you can be in designing your training program, the more likely you will be to meet the requirements of this phase and still ensure enough recovery time. The main purpose of this phase is to get you physically and mentally ready for competition.

A judo match is an anaerobic activity with bouts of work periods lasting 20 to 40 seconds with 10- to 15-second rest periods. Your first priority in the precompetition phase is to develop the ability to push very hard—approximately 85 to 90 percent of your maximum effort—for durations of 20 seconds at first, working up to 40 seconds. If your work time is 40 seconds, rest time is 240 seconds (six times the duration of the work period) when working at 80 to 85 percent of maximum effort. As the duration of work decreases, intensity goes up. Anaerobic training can be achieved by sprinting on a track, using nonspecific exercises, or performing judo specific activities such as speed uchikomi or throwing and groundwork drills with longer rest intervals. If you work for 20 seconds at an intensity of 85 to 90 percent, rest for 120 seconds. If you are new to anaerobic training, I suggest you first attempt nonspecific exercises and then progress to judo specific exercises in stages. Use throws with which you are very familiar. If your form or speed deteriorates, shorten the duration until your fitness increases.

For strength training, the emphasis in this phase is on power and speed endurance. Speed endurance requirements will be met by performing a weight circuit twice a week and by pressure training in lineups at judo twice a week. The maintenance of maximum strength gains is accomplished by maximum strength training once a week and power training four times a week (two or three in judo practice and one or two in the weight room), depending on your weekly schedule. Power and maximum strength training can be combined for one day of maintenance. One session of power training a week will maintain general power. Three sessions a week of specific judo power training will convert that general power into judo-specific power.

Because the goal of this phase is to prepare physically and mentally for competition, you must have a good feel for all the grips, throws, and ground moves you intend to use throughout the competition season. Now is the time to add drills to develop tactics such as speeding up or slowing down the match tempo, fighting in the red zone, or fighting a right- or left-handed fighter combating a grip you find awkward. Ensuring the drills fit within the parameters of a specific energy system, you can develop tactics, mental preparation, and conditioning all in one well-designed drill. Simulation training can be slowly introduced throughout this phase.

To develop judo-specific fitness, perform pressure training twice a week. Line up two to five opponents and fight them one after the other, using both newaza and tachi waza while respecting all the IJF rules of judo. Have someone act as an official to keep the drill intensity high.

Following is a sample week in the precompetition phase:

Day 1: Judo (speed linking skills, tactical drills, controlled randori, simulation fights) and circuit training (strength endurance)

Day 2: Judo (power linking skills, judo-specific skills, lactic acid tolerance drills, controlled randori and hard randori)

Day 3: Off

Day 4: Judo (speed linking skills, tactical drills) and circuit training (strength endurance)

Day 5: Judo (power linking skills, judo-specific lactic acid tolerance drills)

Day 6: Weights (maximum strength and power)

Day 7: Off

Training the anaerobic system requires many short bouts of high-intensity activity as well as many long rest periods. The rest periods should be in the form of active rest. Active rest activity may include very low aerobic exercises at less than 50 percent maximum heart rate, shadow uchikomi, visualization of techniques, or visualization of recovery (getting one's breath back and picturing the muscles eating up lactic acid-replenishing fuels).

Anaerobic exercises have the added benefit of helping you to rehearse staying in the moment. Focus training is also valuable. Try doing simple math problems when fatigued and then have someone ask observational questions about the order in which you fought your opponents in the lineup drill, simple questions about objects in the dojo, or questions about team members, shifting your attention from a narrow focus to a wide focus and back.

Competition or Peaking Phase

The competition phase is the most individualized of all training phases. It relies much more on mental preparation than do the other phases. Because of this, it is very hard to measure improvements or readiness by any objective tests. The only real test or measuring tool is to analyze how you felt and performed on a chosen day. Monitor and record how you prepared for an event and how you felt and performed on the day of the event. Compare these feelings to feelings at other events so over the years you can fine-tune your preparation to meet your specific competitive needs.

The type of competitive season you are planning for will determine your goals during the peaking phase. Your goal may be to compete at peak level in a number of strong competitions, one after another (preferably one week apart). Often such situations are used to gain experience at a higher level of competition than you are used to. These competitions might also be used as a way to qualify for a bigger event, such as the World Championships or the Olympics Games.

The second type of peaking is to perform your best at one major event such as a national championship. This is a much more challenging task. Unlike the previous example, you have only one chance to get it right.

Of course, the two types of peaking can be combined. Because this type of peaking is very difficult to do well, you should attempt it only if you have a lot of experience. You have to keep from peaking at the first event, but because of nervousness, peaking too soon is common.

Over your competitive life, you will have many training cycles. In fact, although I refer to a yearly training program, you can easily adapt the program so you can go through this cycle twice a year or extend it over a 12- to 14-month period. With the first scenario (multiple competitions), you can use the first cycle to qualify for an event, and then peak for a single event on the second time through the cycle. You can fight or go through the four cycles twice a year.

Peaking for Multiple Events

Training to peak for multiple events can last four to six weeks, depending on your experience and preparation. This phase is for competition only, and only maintenance of all the physical and judo components is expected.

Whenever possible, any aerobic training must be of long, slow duration and preferably undertaken in a social or recreational setting to enhance recovery. Aerobic training also can be used as a stress management tool. I recommend two to four 20-minute aerobic workouts a week at no more than 70 percent maximum heart rate (not including warm-up and cool-down). Moderate aerobic exercise such as this is not only beneficial for stress reduction, but also has a strong rejuvenating component.

For strength training, I suggest maximum strength training once every 10 to 14 days with no more than three major exercises with four sets of five repetitions at 70 percent of the maximum single repetition. A strength endurance circuit can be completed once a week, but only if the following weekend doesn't have a competition scheduled. Power and speed will be maintained at judo practice and the judo competition.

Mental preparation includes progressive muscle relaxation seven days a week and visualization seven days a week. Throughout this entire phase, practice good self-talk, concentrating on your strengths and the improvements you have made throughout the year and setting match plans for any shortcomings you noticed during this phase. Also practice staying in the moment!

Judo practice goals are to maintain speed and timing. Practice judo once a week for 1 to 1.5 hours. Include light uchikomi and high-intensity drills that link all aspects of a fight from gripping to groundwork. Allow long rest periods plus one 5-minute lineup with a referee. Make sure you have adequate time for a good warm-up and cool-down.

The weekly schedule for someone training to peak for multiple events might look like this:

Day 1: Competition

Day 2: Light aerobics

Day 3: Off

Day 4: Judo

Day 5: Light aerobics

Day 6: Off or light aerobics

Day 7: Competition

Use your own discretion as to when, or even whether, you do maximum strength training during this phase. If you feel you are not fully recovering from the competitions, then avoid maximum strength training. The strength benefits gained from the act of performing judo itself will maintain a large part of your maximum strength gains over such a short period.

This training schedule may seem light, but remember that the goal of this phase is to enable you to perform to your utmost—to peak! To do that, you must recover fully both physically and mentally from the previous competition. Many judoka try to do both competition tours and training camps during this phase because they naturally want to get the most out of the time and money invested. This kind of concentration is not an efficient way to train because it does not fully commit the judoka to either the goal of competing or the goal of training. Tours of training camps or regular club visits are very useful, but they should be undertaken during the precompetition phase or, better yet, during the cycle or year before you need to peak. It takes six month to a year for the full benefits of such a tour to work their way into your competitive judo, but the experiences and the confidence you gain by competing at your best are valuable and immediate!

Peaking for a Single Event

There are some differences between peaking for multiple events and peaking for a single event. Peaking for multiple events starts during the precompetition phase. When peaking for a single event, you train hard right up until 7 to 10 days before the event. Mental and tactical training must be completed before the final precompetition phase. This is not so when peaking for multiple competitions in which one mental or tactical error does not destroy the whole cycle.

It is easier to design physical training for a single event because you do not have to deal with the physiological stress of a major competition from the week before. By using situation drills, simulation fights, and pressure training in the form of fighting the line, you can fully develop both the tactical and physical aspects of judo in this phase. When peaking for a single event, use the time lines of maintenance requirements of the given energy systems:

Once every 10 days for maximum strength

Once every 10 days for power

Once a week for strength endurance (circuit training)

Twice a week for aerobic fitness

For anaerobic fitness, both the lactic and alactic requirements will be met by tactical judo drills.

You should have four to six judo practices in the final 10 days before a major event. The main goals of these practices are to maintain fitness and timing while reinforcing tactics. Practices must be intense enough to maintain your anaerobic fitness level while still allowing you to recover fully before the event.

A typical 10-day taper might look like this:

Day 10: Maximum strength training

Day 9: Aerobic training (LSD method)

Day 8: Judo

Day 7: Off

Day 6: Off

Day 5: Aerobic training (LSD)

Day 4: Judo

Day 3: Hard judo

Day 2: Judo

Day 1: Aerobic (LSD)

And finally, competition day!

When training to peak for a single event, remember that it is much better to undertrain slightly than it is to overtrain. The mental readiness you gain by being fully rested will make up for any slight level of physical fitness you may lose in the last 10 days before a major event.

12

Focusing for the Match

Judoka deal with the stresses of daily life, school, and family as well as daily or twice-daily training and the stress of getting results in competitions. By any standards, this is a full and busy life that sometimes is exhausting.

You can lessen fatigue by honing your time management skills. Simply by setting priorities and making a schedule, you can see what is possible and what is not within a 24-hour day and 168-hour week. Creating a schedule of the routines of daily life—sleeping, eating, and work or school—and fitting in training times can help you see how much time is left for discretionary events or other commitments.

To be a high-level judoka, you must study time management skills as you would any other aspect of sport. One way to use time efficiently is to cross-train with a recreational activity. The more efficient you can be with your time, the more time you will have. By picking a sport or recreational activity that covers some of your fitness needs and allows you social time as well, you can enjoy the benefits of stress release and include a restorative process—all time well used. Cross-country skiing is a good example. If you take the morning off to cross-country ski with a friend, you meet your aerobic training and social needs. Activity becomes a stress management tool.

This book has covered specific judo skills, different types of conditioning, and strength requirements. It is unrealistic to think that you can train each one of these areas to maximum proficiency or capacity all year long. That's why it is vital to understand which skill or conditioning emphasis takes priority during each phase throughout the year's program (refer to chapter 11). The more you effectively combine two or more aspects of judo training, the more realistic your time commitment to training can be. Remember, the more balanced a life you live throughout the year, the more prepared you will be to push hard at the appropriate times.

PROGRESSIVE MUSCLE RELAXATION

Progressive muscle relaxation (PMR) is an effective technique to help you overcome the stresses that build up throughout the day. As little as 20 minutes of PMR is worth 2 hours of your deepest sleep. Try this technique four to seven days a week.

The most beneficial time to practice PMR is after classes or work, just as you are about to get ready for practice. You will find your energy and focus much more consistent during training after PMR.

Find a comfortable place to sit or lie down. With your eyes closed, take three large breaths, expanding your abdomen as you inhale. As you exhale, simply repeat in your mind that you give yourself permission to let go of all tensions. With each exhale, say to yourself, I'm in a warm, safe environment, and I give myself permission to let go.

Now bring your attention to your hands. Make two fists. Notice the growing tension in your hands, wrists, and forearms. Bend your wrists. Notice how the tension moves up the forearms. Bend your elbows, contracting your biceps and triceps, and hold the tension for 3 seconds. Now let go of all the tension in the arms and recognize the sensation of letting go. Repeat once.

Bring your attention to your shoulders. Shrug your shoulders up to your ears as much as possible. If you are lying down, push the back of your head lightly into the ground. Notice the tension in your neck. Squeeze your shoulder blades together, letting go of any tightness or tension across your upper chest. Hold for 3 seconds. Notice the tension in the shoulder girdle and neck and simply let go. Repeat once more.

Bring your attention to your abdomen. Suck in your abdomen, imagining that your belly button is touching your spine. Now suck your belly button up under your rib cage, creating as much tension in your abdomen as possible. Hold the tension for 3 seconds and let it go.

Bring your attention to your lower body. Pointing your toes away from your head, push your heels into the ground and contract your calves, hamstrings, thighs, and glutes. If you are lying down, push your lower back flat into the ground. Feel the tension through the whole lower body. Hold that tension for 3 seconds and then simply let go of all the tension. Repeat.

Now bring your attention to your face. We often carry a lot of tension in our faces and jaws. Mentally connect with the muscles around the face, starting with the jaw. Slightly part your lips. Notice how that relieved the tension in the jaw. Now bring your attention to the muscle above your eyebrows and cheeks. Imagine those muscles letting go of all tension. With that letting go, all the tension simply melts away.

As you enjoy the sensation of release, scan your body for muscles that are resistant to letting go of tension. Contract them for 3 seconds and then let go of the tension.

Concentrate on your normal breathing. With each exhale, allow your body to sink deeper into the floor or chair. Lie or sit there for the next 15 minutes just enjoying the sensation of letting go.

You may find it helpful to read these instructions into a tape recorder, allowing approximately 5 to 10 seconds for each muscle group and repetition, until you memorize the order.

MATCH FOCUS

The prematch relaxation process must start long before competition. By staying in the moment, you can control wasteful nervous energy during preparation. This in turn reduces fatigue from worry and disturbed rest and allows you to perform the task that is most beneficial at that moment in preparing for the upcoming competition. This skill of staying in the moment is very beneficial in the fast pace of a judo match.

During both competition and training, the ability to stay in the moment is crucial. *Staying in the moment* is simply a phrase to describe concentrating on what's happening in the moment. Some athletes have this ability naturally. Distractions and other projects or goals seem to disappear when they are training or competing. For those of us who were not so fortunate as to be born with this skill, luckily it is trainable. But we must practice it during training before we can expect it to appear magically during competition.

A successful judoka is able to stay in the moment during a match.

You can take the first step toward developing the ability to stay in the moment at practice. Set a short-term goal for each phase of practice. The more specific an immediate goal, the easier it is to focus on its completion. The short-term goal of each phase should contribute to the completion of a larger goal.

Imagine that you are anticipating a practice in which you will get to use a new throw or ground move. At the practice, you concentrate so much on this new throw or move that you don't give the proper attention to your warm-up and to your mental or physical preparation for randori. You start the randori focused only on the throw, without the important links that lead up to the goal. Suddenly you find that you cannot achieve the throw. You tell yourself that you are having an off night, starting a downward spiral of negative thinking. You convince yourself that you are having a terrible practice.

Now consider the opposite path. You come to practice and concentrate on each phase of practice. You start randori without a preconceived throw to use. You focus on obtaining your grip, then on circling, creating an automatic and successful throw. Even if you didn't feel like coming to practice at first, you end up glad that you came to this great practice.

For each stage in practice, ask yourself this simple question: Is what I am doing at this moment contributing to my final goal in the best way possible?

For each randori, begin by reminding yourself of the links: grip, circle, entry, and attack. When there is a break in the action, breathe to replace oxygen debt. Take two short, hard sniffs and one hard, forced exhale. Repeat three times and then go back to breathing normally. Each time you hear the word *matte*, repeat this sequence in your head: grips, circle, entry, attack, transition to newaza. Breathe, assessing the situation as you get back. Walk to the line knowing clearly whether you are winning or losing and how much time is left in the match. Decide on any adjustments you must make. Once you are back on the starting line, cue yourself to start the sequence automatically, telling yourself, I must get my grip! The rest of the sequence will automatically play out.

SIMULATIONS

Simulations are dress rehearsals for competition, but they can be manipulated to emphasize situations or conditions that you find challenging. In simulations, the focus is on performance rather than winning or losing, whereas drills have prearranged actions and outcomes. Simulations flow much more freely and are more situational than drills are. Simulation exercises should be used during the late precompetition phase.

The simplest examples are best: If you do not like the pressure of fighting in front of friends and family, you might ask some chosen friends and family members to come to the club to watch you in some friendly club matches against your teammates. Adding the stressor of family to the club match adds a whole new and helpful dimension. It would also be appropriate to combine this situation with focusing on staying in the moment. If before the match starts you begin to worry about how you will appear to your friends and family, simply ask yourself, Does this action best contribute to my final goal? Obviously, worrying does not, so a more appropriate action would be to do a relaxation exercise, if time allows, or to concentrate more strongly on the warm-up.

These are just two examples of how simulations can assist in overcoming a specific weakness in competition. Following are other situations that can be set up as simulation exercises:

- Fighting from behind with a specific score
- Fighting when winning with a specific score
- Losing your head because of perceived bad officiating
- Dealing with pressure from family and friends
- Fighting when fatigued

Victory is sweet for those who have trained for it.

Senior judoka should have upwards of 50 matches a year. For many of us that would be a very difficult number of matches to achieve. By using realistic simulations, you can add a large number of these dress rehearsals to achieve the goal of 50. To count as a match, each simulation fight must follow all the rules of judo and must have an importance, a significance for you. Simulations are excellent and often underused tools in preparing for major competitions.

PREMATCH FOCUS AND AROUSAL

The morning of the competition is always a busy and stressful time. It consists of an early morning weigh-in, breakfast, and rushing to the shia-jo (tournament hall), often after a restless or poor night's sleep! This is not a good combination for maximum performance. Often those who can handle the situation best are the ones who make it through the first few rounds of the tournament.

Preparation for your first match is vitally important. Relaxation exercises such as PMR can be of great benefit in overcoming the fatigue of a restless night and the stress of competition day. PMR exercises must be done a minimum of 1 hour before competition.

Staying in the moment really comes into play when preparing for matches. Throughout the day while waiting for matches to begin, question what you are doing, asking, Is this the best thing for achieving the final outcome? Sitting worrying about your draw or opponent is pointless. Performing a relaxation exercise, drinking liquids, going over a match plan with the coach, or stretching and staying loose are all vital and productive. Nervousness and stress often create fatigue and lethargy. Light aerobic exercise such as brisk walking around the tournament area often alleviates these symptoms. Understanding how nerves affect the body and its energy levels will help you control nervousness.

An appropriate warm-up is often the simplest and most effective tool for creating the perfect arousal level for maximum performance. A hard warm-up for approximately 2.5 minutes (approximately half the match) performed no less than 10 minutes before the first match can work wonders. This does not include light aerobic exercises, stretching, or light uchikomi, but may include hard grip fighting and hard newaza. If no partner is available, try hard interval running; if you are familiar with interval skipping or sets of power uchikomi, using inner tubes is a good alternative.

Traditionally, athletes are superstitious by nature; they try to find every small advantage to help convince themselves they will win. Good luck charms are fine because you have control over them. However, avoid relying on good luck charms or favorite situations such as always fighting in the blue gi or having a friend watching to bring good luck. You may not always have control over these things. Rituals such as crossing yourself before you fight, stomping your feet at the side of a mat like a sumo fighter, rubbing your ears, or slapping your face are under your control and can be used as cues that now is the time to fight.

How you talk to yourself while waiting to go out and fight is also important. All fighters have some self-doubt on the day of competition. With that self-doubt should come a much larger belief in yourself. This belief in yourself is what you must focus on. The more you can focus on your strengths and attributes, the less self-doubt can creep in. Thinking of tasks that must be done throughout the fight and going over checklists in your mind reinforces your confidence and communicates to your subconscious that the hours of drills and randori have prepared you for any situation. There is a lot of truth in the old saying, If you think you can, you might. If you think you can't, you won't.

Index

Note: The italicized *f* and *t* refer to figures and tables, respectively.

About the Author

Ron Angus is a 5th degree black belt who has practiced judo for 42 years and has taught and studied the sport in more than 15 countries. As a competitor, Angus represented Canada at one Commonwealth Game and three Commonwealth Championships, and he was a 10-time World Masters Champion. He has competed in 23 consecutive Senior Nationals, 22 Canadian Nationals, and one British National Championship.

As the New Zealand National Team North American Project coach from 1984 to 1996, Angus led teams to three World Championships and to the 1996 Olympic Games. In addition, he has produced both national and international champions in judo, sambo, and grappling.

Angus is currently a motivational speaker on the topics of fitness and mental well being for the Canadian-based Alliance Fitness Corporation. He is also a National Coaching Course Program (NCCP) instructor, the NCCP Judo Ontario Chairman, and a member of Judo Canada's Coaching Diffusion Committee, which shares coaching principles with fellow coaches.

Angus and his wife, Tracy, reside in Burlington, Ontario, Canada. You can learn more about them, the Full Circle Judo Club, and competitive judo at their Web site, www.fullcirclejudoclub.ca.